MW00609887

Pass Publications LLC

FINRA Series 7 Exam / Mastering Options:
500 Options Practice Exam Questions & Full Explanations
(Volumes I & II)

Table of Contents

About Pass Publications – I   iv

Structure of the Series 7 Exam – II   v

Options and the Series 7 Exam –II   v

How to Use This Manual – III   vi

Learning Method vs. Testing Method - III   vi

Options Exam 1   1

Options Explanations 1   7

Options Exam 2   19

Options Explanations 2   25

Options Exam 3   38

Options Explanations 3   44

Options Exam 4   57

Options Explanations 4   63

Options Exam 5   74

Options Explanations 5   81

Options Exam 6   91

Options Explanations 6   97

Options Exam 7   108

Options Explanations 7   114

Options Exam 8   126

Options Explanations 8   132

Options Exam 9   145

Options Explanations 9   151

Options Exam 10   163

Options Explanations 10   169

About Pass Publications

Mr. Andrew S. Klick is the Founder and content author of Pass Publications. From the beginning, his objective was to create highly targeted and effective study materials designed to compliment a student's core study program.

Mr. Klick has 24 years of combined compliance, brokerage, and securities training experience. He has trained thousands of students for FINRA exam preparation courses while employed by various training vendors. Most notably, from 2002 to 2006, Mr. Klick was a founder and the Senior Course Designer of CCH Wall Street Financial Training, Inc. He conducted research, developed classroom presentations, online training programs, and textbooks for the Series 7, 6, 24, 26, 9-10, 63, 65, 66, and 87 exams. His international teaching experience includes Australia, China, England, India, Italy, Japan, and Switzerland.

In addition to his responsibilities at Pass Publications, Mr. Klick is the Chief Compliance Officer for a Manhattan based broker-dealer. He holds the Series 7 and 24 licenses, and is a graduate of the University of Maryland.

Structure of the Series 7 Exam

The Series 7 Exam (General Securities Representative) consists of 250 graded questions. In addition, students will see 10 experimental questions for a total of 260 questions. Experimental questions are not identified as such, so students must attempt to answer each and every question correctly.

The exam is divided into two sessions. In the first session, students have 185 minutes to complete 130 multiple-choice questions. Again, in the second session, students have 185 minutes to complete an additional 130 multiple-choice questions. The test is graded as a single exam following completion of the second session. The passing score is 72%. For more information, please visit: www.finra.org

Options and the Series 7 Exam

Options are the most heavily tested topic on the Series 7 Exam. Options questions account for approximately 20% of the exam (50 questions). While this is a very broad exam, requiring competency in many different areas, it is critical that students have a mastery of options to be successful. Our practice exams cover the entire spectrum of options questions that you may encounter on the Series 7 exam.

How to Use This Manual

This manual is designed to supplement your core study program. The manual has been divided into 10 options practice exams containing 50 questions each, with a total of 500 questions. Each exam is followed by full explanations. Make sure you take the time to read each explanation to heighten your understanding of each question. All exams were designed to be of equal difficultly level and to simulate the questions you may encounter on the Series 7 Exam.

It is best to incorporate these options exams into your core study program. One method we recommend is to complete Options Exam 1 then go back to your core study program to complete a properly weighted exam. You may then decide to complete two options exams before returning to your core study program to complete a properly weighted exam. The idea is to rotate between an options exam(s) and a properly weighted exam.

Learning Method vs. Testing Method

Each exam can be taken using the Learning Method or Testing Method, both of which have their advantages and disadvantages.

Utilizing the Learning Method, read the question and then go immediately to the answer. Make sure you read the full explanation. The advantage of this method is that each question is fresh in your mind, allowing for greater comprehension of each concept. The disadvantage is that this method can be very time consuming.

With the Testing Method, your focus is on simulating the exam taking process. For example, beginning with Options Exam 1, you complete the full 50-question exam before reviewing any of the explanations. You should allow yourself 70 minutes to complete the entire exam. After completing the exam, you then review each answer/explanation. The advantage of this method is that it is generally less time consuming than the Learning Method and more closely simulates the exam taking process. The disadvantage is that each question is not as fresh in your mind, making comprehension of each concept less effective than the Learning Method.

This is not an exact science, and you need to decide which method may work best for you. Take into consideration your understanding of the topic and any time constraints which you may have.

OPTIONS EXAM 1

1. Jack buys 1,000 MSFT at $25 and also purchases 10 MSFT May 20 puts for 2. The best possible outcome for Jack would be if MSFT stock experienced:

   (A) high volatility.
   (B) low volatility.
   (C) a major decline.
   (D) a major increase.

2. An investor purchases a T-Note Dec 95 straddle for a total premium of 6.19. At which two of the following prices would the investor break even?

   I.   101.59
   II. 88.81
   III. 101.19
   IV. 88.13

   (A) I and II
   (B) I and IV
   (C) II and III
   (D) III and IV

3. A Debit Put Spread can be created from which two of the following?

   I.   Long 1 XYZ Nov 80 put
   II. Short 1 XYZ Nov 80 put
   III. Long 1 XYZ Nov 85 put
   IV. Short 1 XYZ Nov 85 put

   (A) I and III
   (B) I and IV
   (C) II and III
   (D) II and IV

4. The Ford Mar 15 call options is an example of a:

   (A) Class
   (B) Type
   (C) Strategy
   (D) Series

5. Which of the following is the method of settlement for index options?

   (A) Physical settlement
   (B) Any method deemed fair and reasonable
   (C) Exchange for physicals
   (D) Cash settlement

6. Eddie sells 5 GHI Nov 20 calls at 2 and also sells 5 GHI Nov 20 puts at 2. What is Eddie's maximum loss?

   (A) Unlimited
   (B) $2,000
   (C) $1,000
   (D) $4,000

7. Bob buys an Apr 55 put on the 30-year T-bond yield for 3. At expiration, the yield on the 30-year T-bond's yield is at 5.85%. The resulting profit or loss is:

   (A) $350 profit
   (B) $50 profit
   (C) $300 loss
   (D) $350 loss

8. Gary goes long 5 XON Oct 75 calls at a premium of 5. With XON stock trading at $73, how much time value do the call options have?

   (A) 3 points
   (B) 5 points
   (C) 2 points
   (D) 0 points

9. An investor created the following position:

    Bought 1 XOM Dec 35 put
    Sold 1 XOM Dec 40 put

    Which two of the following characteristics are TRUE of this position?

    I.   Credit
    II. Debit
    III. The investor expects the spread to narrow
    IV. The investor expects the spread to widen

    (A) I and III
    (B) I and IV
    (C) II and III
    (D) II and IV

10. A customer places an initial trade to buy 5 ABC Aug 50 calls at 5. The branch office which maintains the customer's account does not receive an executed customer agreement within the allotted time. Which of the following orders may the RR accept from the customer?

    (A) Buy 5 ABC Aug 50 calls
    (B) Sell 5 ABC Aug 50 calls
    (C) Buy 5 ABC Aug 55 calls
    (D) Sell 5 ABC Aug 55 calls

11. A customer of Brokerage Capital Inc. decides to buy 10 ABC Nov 70 puts at 5. What is the customer's percentage margin requirement?

    (A) 50%
    (B) 25%
    (C) 0%
    (D) 100%

12. An investor exercises an IBM June 50 put at 3. For tax purposes, what is the investor's sales proceeds?

    (A) $5,300
    (B) $5,000
    (C) $4,700
    (D) $5,000

13. Which one of the following is a correct statement regarding the adjustment of an options contract for a cash dividend? The exercise price is:

    (A) unchanged.
    (B) cancelled.
    (C) decreased.
    (D) increased.

14. An investor goes long 1 ABC June 40 put at 7. What is his maximum potential loss?

    (A) $3,000
    (B) Unlimited
    (C) $700
    (D) $4,700

15. Which one of the following is NOT a characteristic of a Covered Call Writing Strategy?

    (A) Conservative strategy
    (B) Can only be implemented in a cash account
    (C) The writer will have a short-term capital gain if the option expires worthless
    (D) An income-generating strategy

16. On March 15, 2010, Frank bought 1 XON Oct 50 call at 5. On October 20, 2010, the XON option expires worthless. For tax purposes, Frank has a $500:

    (A) short-term capital loss.
    (B) short-term ordinary loss.
    (C) long-term capital loss.
    (D) long-term ordinary loss.

17. An investor exercises an IBM June 50 call. According to industry regulations, when does settlement take place?

    (A) T + 3
    (B) T + 5
    (C) T + 1
    (D) T + 2

18. Jack buys 1 XYZ Aug 30 put at 5. What is Jack's maximum potential gain?

    (A) Unlimited
    (B) $5,000
    (C) $2,500
    (D) $3,000

19. Which one of the four strategies has unlimited loss potential?

    (A) Long straddle
    (B) Short straddle
    (C) Vertical spread
    (D) Covered call

20. Who determines the premiums paid by investors for options that trade on the CBOE?

    (A) CBOE
    (B) Market forces
    (C) Options market makers
    (D) OCC

21. An investor goes short 10 XYZ May 25 puts at 3. What is his maximum potential gain?

    (A) $300
    (B) $22,000
    (C) $2,200
    (D) $3,000

22. In a cash account, Ed goes long 100 shares of IBM at $42 and also goes short 1 IBM Aug 45 call at a premium of 3. What is Ed's margin requirement?

    (A) $4,500
    (B) 44,800
    (C) $3,900
    (D) $4,200

23. An investor places a market order to buy an XYZ Nov 35 put which is trading at 4.15 - 4.25. One month later she liquidates her position when the options are trading at 4.35 - 4.55. What is the investor's resulting profit?

    (A) $25 profit
    (B) $40 profit
    (C) $10 profit
    (D) $20 profit

24. Why would an investor write a Straddle? He:

    (A) expects volatility.
    (B) expects neutrality.
    (C) is bullish.
    (D) is bearish.

25. Ford stock is currently trading at $15.75. Which one of the following options is in-the-money?

    (A) Aug 20 calls
    (B) Aug 15 puts
    (C) Nov 20 puts
    (D) Nov 25 calls

26. Joan initiates a position with the purchase of an Apr 30 put at 3. This is an example of:

    (A) a closing purchase.
    (B) a closing sale.
    (C) an opening sale.
    (D) an opening purchase.

27. Martin manages the Preferred Stock Plus mutual fund. Which two of the following could be utilized to best hedge his portfolio?

    I.   Long yield-based call options
    II. Long interest rate call options
    III. Long yield-based put options
    IV. Long interest rate put options

    (A) I and II
    (B) I and IV
    (C) II and III
    (D) II and IV

28. Gary purchases 1,000 shares of XYZ at $50.75, and at the same time also purchases 10 XYZ Nov 50 puts at 3. In November the puts expire worthless and Gary sells the stock for $52. Which two of the following statements are correct?

    I.   Gary's cost basis on the stock is $53.75
    II. Gary's cost basis on the stock is $50.75
    III. Gary's sales proceeds on the stock are $52
    IV. Gary's sales proceeds on the stock are $49

    (A) I and III
    (B) I and IV
    (C) II and III
    (D) II and IV

29. Kent goes short 3 QYZ Feb 80 puts at 3, and 3 QYZ Feb 75 calls at 6.5. What is Kent's expectation of the underlying stock between now and February?

    (A) Stability
    (B) Volatility
    (C) Bullish
    (D) Bearish

30. In his brokerage account, an investor is short 1 DEF June 65 put. The addition of which one of the following positions would create a short straddle? Write 1:

    (A) DEF June 65 call
    (B) DEF July 65 call
    (C) DEF June 60 call
    (D) DEG June 65 call

31. An investor goes long 10 XDC (Canadian Dollar) Dec 105 calls for 3.14 and later sells them for 2.11. What is the resulting profit or loss?

    (A) $103 profit
    (B) $103 loss
    (C) $1,030 profit
    (D) $1,030 loss

32. Patrick purchases a DEF May 55 put for $400 when the underlying stock is trading at $57. What is the intrinsic value of the put option?

    (A) $0
    (B) $400
    (C) $200
    (D) -$200

33. Taleen bought 100 shares of GHI at $40. She also bought 1 GHI Apr 35 put at 2. At what price does GHI stock need to trade for Taleen to earn a profit?

    (A) $42
    (B) $43
    (C) $33
    (D) $32

34. Claudia purchased 3 XON Sept 60 puts at 5 and wrote 3 XON Sept 65 puts at 8. At what price would Claudia breakeven?

    (A) $57
    (B) $62
    (C) $68
    (D) $55

35. An investor buys 1 XYZ Oct 60 put at 3, and sells 1 XYZ Oct 55 put at 2. What is the investor's margin requirement?

    (A) $100
    (B) $300
    (C) $500
    (D) $200

36. An investor expects the Federal Reserve Board to tighten interest rates. Which two of the following option positions would be consistent with his outlook?

    I.   Long yield-based call options
    II. Short yield-based call options
    III. Long yield-based put options
    IV. Short yield-based put options

    (A) I and III
    (B) I and IV
    (C) II and III
    (D) II and IV

37. A trader is long 60,000 DEF call options. 100,000 contracts is the position limit for DEF. Which of the following additional positions would be permissible?

    (A) 45,000 short puts
    (B) 42,000 long calls
    (C) 65,000 long puts
    (D) 105,000 short calls

38. Nancy buys a Feb 55 call based on the 30-year T-bond yield for 3. At expiration, the 30-year T-bond's yield is at 5.85%. The resulting profit or loss is:

    (A) $350 profit
    (B) $50 profit
    (C) $350 loss
    (D) $50 loss

39. Tony writes 10 XYZ Oct 30 calls at 3.50, and also writes 10 XYZ Oct 30 puts at 3. What is Tony's maximum loss?

    (A) $3,500
    (B) $3,000
    (C) $6,500
    (D) Unlimited

40. Which one of the following terms defines the number of outstanding option contracts in a particular option series?

    (A) Open interest
    (B) Volume
    (C) Liquidity
    (D) Size

41. Which of the following activities takes place last when opening an options account?

    (A) Account approval by an ROP
    (B) Execution of a trade
    (C) RR determines suitability
    (D) ODD is sent to the customer

42. An investor writes 1 KO Mar 65 put and also writes 1 KO Mar 60 call. The investor has engaged in which of the following strategies?

    (A) Diagonal spread
    (B) Price spread
    (C) Short straddle
    (D) Short combination

43. An investor establishes the following position:

    Short 5 XOM Apr 75 puts at 5
    Long 5 XOM Apr 80 puts at 8

    In April, both options expire worthless. What is the investor's profit or loss?

    (A) $1,500 loss
    (B) $1,500 profit
    (C) $300 loss
    (D) $300 profit

44. Janice just wrote a DEF Nov 55 call at 5. In which of the following scenarios would Janice achieve her maximum gain? At expiration, DEF stock is trading:

    I.   below its strike price
    II. above its strike price
    III. at its strike price

    (A) I only
    (B) II only
    (C) I and III only
    (D) II and III only

45. Pam goes long 1 XYZ May 40 put at 3 and 1 XYZ May 45 call at 4.5. What is Pam's maximum loss?

   (A) $750
   (B) Unlimited
   (C) $450
   (D) $300

46. Which one of the following is a correct statement regarding the adjustment of an options contract for an odd stock split? The number of contracts is:

   (A) increased.
   (B) decreased.
   (C) cancelled.
   (D) unchanged.

47. Paul writes 1 XYZ Mar 65 put at 3 and also writes 1 XYZ Mar 60 call at 5. At which two of the following prices does the underlying stock need to trade for Paul to break even?

   I. $57
   II. $68
   III. $62
   IV. $65

   (A) I and II
   (B) I and III
   (C) II and III
   (D) III and IV

48. A speculator anticipates the dollar will weaken against the Euro. Which two of the following strategies could the speculator use to profit from his expectation?

   I.   Buy puts on the Euro
   II. Buy calls on the Euro
   III. Sell calls on the Euro
   IV. Sell puts on the Euro

   (A) I and II
   (B) I and III
   (C) II and III
   (D) II and IV

49. Rodney Rich has a $5 million stock portfolio that he expects to decline in value over the next three to six months. He would like to hedge his portfolio with the S&P 500 (SPX) 1250 puts. His portfolio has a beta of 1.2 and the value of the SPX Index is 1293. How many put options will he need to purchase to properly hedge his portfolio?

   (A) 46
   (B) 38
   (C) 40
   (D) 48

50. A credit call spread can be created from which two of the following?

   I.   Long 1 ABC Oct 80 call
   II. Short 1 ABC Oct 80 call
   III. Long 1 ABC Oct 85 call
   IV. Short 1 ABC Oct 85 call

   (A) I and III
   (B) I and IV
   (C) II and III
   (D) II and IV

OPTIONS EXPLANATIONS 1

1. **(D)**

The position is a Protective Put Purchase which consists of a long stock position and a long put(s). Jack is using the long puts as an insurance policy to protect against a decline in his long stock position.

The best possible outcome for Jack would be a major increase in MSFT stock. In theory, MSFT stock could increase to an infinite price, yielding Jack an unlimited gain on the stock. In this scenario, Jack would not exercise his put options, and as a result, would only lose the $2,000 premium he paid for the puts options.

When creating a Protective Put position, an investor's maximum potential gain is unlimited and would be realized from an infinite rise in the stock. Again, the put option(s) is only purchased as an insurance policy in the event of a decline in the price of the stock.

2. **(D)**

A Straddle consists of the purchase or sale of a call and a put, same security, expiration dates, and strike prices. So, this position can be rewritten as:

| Buy 1 T-Note Dec 95 call |
| Buy 1 T-Note Dec 95 put |

While we do not know what the premium is for the put or the call individually, we do know that the total premium paid for both the put and the call is 6.19. It is important to note that a straddle has two breakeven points. The breakeven points for the straddle are:

Strike Price of Call	+ Total Premium	= Upside Breakeven Point
Strike Price of Put	-Total Premium	= Downside Breakeven Point

Therefore, breakeven points are:

Strike Price of Call	+ Total Premium	= Upside Breakeven Point
95	+ 6.19	= 101.19

Strike Price of Put	-Total Premium	= Downside Breakeven Point
95	-6.19	= 88.13

An investor that buys a straddle is neither bullish nor bearish. Instead the investor that buys a straddle expects volatility in the underlying security. So, the investor expects the T-Note's price to go above 101.19 (upside breakeven) or to go below 88.13 (downside breakeven).

3. **(C)**

A Debit Put Spread can be created by going short (writing) 1 XYZ Nov 80 put, and going long (buying) 1 XYZ Nov 85 put. While no premiums are given in the question, the put option with the higher strike price will have a higher premium given the same expiration dates. Since the XYZ 80 has been written, and the XYZ 85 put has been purchased, the investor would pay out more money than has been received. As a result, the investor would be a "net buyer" or have a net debit spread. Ideally, the investor wants to see a large decline in XYZ stock which would translate to a widening of the spread.

4. **(D)**

Let us start by first defining Type, Class, and Series. A type divides the options universe into calls and puts. An example of a Type includes all calls or all puts. A class consists of the same type and same security. An example of a class would be all calls on Ford or all puts on Microsoft. A Series consists of the same security (Ford), same expiration date (March), same strike price (15), and same type (call). So, the Ford Mar 15 calls is an example of a series. You may think of a Series as being the most specific of the terms type, class, and series.

5. **(D)**

Index options utilize a cash settlement. Let us review an example:

Susan buys an SPX (S&P 500 index) Oct 1250 call. Two weeks later, Susan exercises her call option when the underlying index is at 1255. Susan will receive the intrinsic value or in-the-money value in cash. The writer or seller which received an assignment notice will pay Susan $500 which can be determined as follows:

Intrinsic Value in points	X number of contracts	X contract size	= $ Intrinsic Value
5	X 1	X 100	= $500

Physical settlement (choice A) is utilized by equity options. Any method deemed fair and reasonable (choice B) refers to an allocation method for assignment notices to writers of options. Exchange for physicals (choice C) is not a term that is applicable to the Series 7 exam.

6. **(A)**

The straddle writer is short both a call(s) and a put(s) on the same security, same expiration dates, and same strike prices. The key concept is that embedded in the straddle writer's position is a naked or uncovered call option. It is the naked call option that lends the position to unlimited risk. Theoretically, the underlying stock could rise to infinity. The call option would be exercised by the buyer. This means the straddle writer would receive an assignment notice which would trigger the obligation to sell the stock at the strike price. Since the straddle writer does not own the underlying stock, he would first need to purchase the underlying security in the market at an infinite price, and then sell the underlying security at the strike price.

Like the naked call writer, the straddle writer has unlimited risk, and is only suitable for investors that are willing to assume such risk.

7. **(C)**

Bob has purchased a yield-based put option. The buyer of a yield-based option is speculating on the direction of the yield or interest rate as opposed to the price. Bob expects the yield on the 30-year T-bond to fall below 5.5% (to determine the yield, simply divide the strike price by 10. (55/10 = 5.5% yield)

Since the yield of the underlying 30-year T-bond is above 5.5% at expiration, the put option expire is worthless. Just like the buyer of any option, the maximum loss is the purchase price or debit paid for the option. Bob initially paid $300 for the option. Therefore his maximum loss would be $300 which can be determined as follows:

Premium	X Number of contracts	X Contract Size	= $Premium
3	X 1	X 100	= $300

8.   **(B)**

The Time Value of an option is determined as follows:

Option Premium	– Intrinsic Value	= Time Value

So, first we need to determine if the option has any intrinsic value or money value. A call option is in-the-money if the exercise price or strike price is below the market price of the underlying stock. Since the exercise price is above the market price, the option has zero intrinsic value (note, there is no such thing as negative intrinsic value). Now let us go back to our example:

Option Premium	– Intrinsic Value	= Time Value
5	0	= 5

The key is to first determine whether or not an option has intrinsic value before attempting to determine the options time value. Whatever amount remains is the time value.

9.   **(A)**

The first step is being able to identify that this is a net credit spread or simply a credit spread Even though no premiums are given in this question, you can determine that the put option with the higher strike price has a higher premium (since the expiration dates are the same).

The investor writes or sells the 40 put which brings in more money that is paid out for the 35 put. As a result, the investor is a "net seller" or has established a net credit spread. Ideally, a net creditor or would like both options to expire worthless.

Let us expand on this by using some hypothetical numbers. For example, an investor sold the 40 put for a premium of 5 and bought the 35 put for 3. The investor has a net credit of 2. The goal of a net creditor or writer would be for the options to expire worthless. In other words, he would like the spread to go to zero by expiration. If the spread was established at a net credit of 2 and expires at zero, the spread is said to narrow; go from a higher number to a lower number.

10. **(B)**

Since an executed customer agreement was not received within the allotted time, the customer may only engage in closing transactions. In other words, the customer may only liquidate his existing position. Since the customer initiated his position with an opening purchase of 5 ABC Aug 50 calls, he may only engage in a closing sale by selling 5 ABC Aug 50 calls.

11. **(D)**

The Federal Reserve Board controls the extension of credit by broker-dealers, which is governed by Regulation T. The buyer of an option is required to deposit the full premium or 100% when purchasing an option. To determine the premium in dollars, we can utilize the following formula:

Premium	x Number of Contracts	x Contract Size	= $Premium
5	x 10	x 100	= $5,000

The customer will need to deposit 100% of the premium or $5,000.

12. **(C)**

For tax purposes, the investor's sales proceeds are $4,700. For determining the sales proceeds, the following formula can be applied:

Aggregate Exercise Price of Put	-Premium	= Sales Proceeds
$5,000	-$300	= $4,700

To summarize, the investor exercised the put in which she sold the stock at the strike price of 50. However, the investor paid a $300 premium for the put option which is then subtracted from the sales proceeds.

13. **(A)**

The exercise price or strike price is not adjusted for cash dividends. It is important to remember that adjustments to the strike price of an option contract is made for stock dividends, even stock splits, and odd stock splits.

14. **(C)**

An investor that purchases an option (whether a put or call) has limited loss potential. The loss is limited to the debit or the premium paid for the option. To determine the total debit or premium paid, we can apply the following formula:

Premium	X number of contracts	X contract size	= $Premium
7	X 1	X 100	= $700

15. **(B)**

The covered call writer is long stock and writes or sells a call on the underlying stock. Note, this is an "Except" question which means that three of the four choices are true. The correct answer is the false choice. The correct answer, which is false, is "B". Covered call writing can be implemented in both a cash account and margin account. Let us review an example to best understand why the other choices are true. An investor creates the following position:

Buy 100 ABC at $50
Write 1 ABC Oct 55 call at 3

This is a conservative strategy (choice A) because the maximum loss is the amount paid for the stock minus the premium received for writing the option. The maximum loss is $4,700.

The writer will have a short-term capital gain if the option expire is worthless. This is a true statement since the maximum expiration of a standard or regular option is nine months, making it short term since it does not exceed twelve months. Options are also a capital asset, so the receipt of any premium would make it a short-term capital gain if the option expires worthless.

This is also an income-generating strategy (choice D), as the call is written to generate income. This is also a popular strategy with dividend paying stocks. The investor receives dividend income from the underlying stock in addition to the premium income received for writing the call option.

16. **(A)**

Frank realized a short-term capital loss of $500. Standardized options have a maximum life of nine (9) months. Since a holding period of twelve (12) months or less results in short-term gains or losses, the result is a short-term capital gain or short term capital loss.

17. **(A)**

It is important to read the question very carefully. The question begins by stating that an investor "exercises" a call option. When the investor exercises the IBM June 50 call, he is purchasing the stock at $50/share (strike price). Since this is a purchase of stock, settlement takes place three days following the trade date.

If instead, the question began by reading, "An investor 'purchases' an IBM June 50 call," settlement would take place within one day following the trade date (T+1).

18. **(C)**

As the buyer of a put, Jack's maximum potential gain would be realized if the stock fell to zero. If the market for XYZ stock fell to zero, Jack could buy the stock at $0/share and exercise his put, putting or selling the stock to the writer at the strike price of $30/share. Jack's profit would be 30 points less the 5 point premium paid for the put or $2,500. The put buyer's maximum gain can be determined by applying the following formula:

Aggregate Exercise Price	-Premium	= Maximum Gain
$3,000	-$500	= $2,500

19. **(B)**

A short straddle (straddle writer) is short (writes) both a call and a put on the same security, same expiration dates, and same strike prices. The key concept is that embedded in the straddle writer's position is a naked call option. It is the naked call option that lends the position to unlimited risk. Theoretically, the underlying stock could rise to infinity. The call option would then be exercised by the buyer. This means the straddle writer would receive an assignment notice which would trigger the obligation to sell the stock at the strike price. Since the straddle writer does not own the underlying stock, it would first need to be purchased in the market at an infinite price, and then sold at the strike price. Like the naked call writer, the straddle writer has unlimited risk, and is only suitable for investors that are willing to assume such risk.

20. **(B)**

Premiums are determined by market forces or the forces of supply and demand.

The Options Clearing Corporation ("OCC") issues and guarantees all option contracts. The following features are standardized by the OCC:

- Security
- Strike Price
- Expiration date.

The premium is not standardized, but determined by market forces.

21. **(D)**

As the writer of a put, the investor's maximum potential gain would be limited to the premium received. The put writer's maximum gain in dollars can be determined by using the following formula:

Premium	X number of contracts	X contract size	= $Premium
3	X 10	X 100	= $3,000

22. **(D)**

You should be able to identify the position as a covered call writing strategy, which consists of a long stock position and a short call option.

The term "covered" in this context, means "covered for margin purposes", which means that no margin deposit is required on the sale of option. In a cash account, the investor would be required to deposit 100% of the purchase price of the stock, or $4,200. If instead this transaction took place in a margin account, the required deposit would be 50% of the price of the stock or $1,100.

23. **(C)**

In the first scenario, the XYZ Nov 35 put is trading at 4.15 – 4.25. The 4.15 refers to the bid, the price at which the market maker is willing to buy the option. The 4.25 refers to the ask, which is the price at which the market maker is willing to sell the option. Since the investor is not a market maker, she would purchase the option at the higher of the two prices (ask price), and sell the option at the lower of the two prices (bid price). Let us take a closer look at both scenarios:

Transaction	Trading	Price Bought or Sold	Debit or Credit
Bought 1 XYZ Nov 35 put	4.15 - 4.25	4.25	-$425 debit
Sold 1 XYZ Nov 35 put	4.35 - 4.55	4.35	+$435 credit
$10 profit			

24. **(B)**

The straddle writer is short both a call(s) and a put(s) on the same security, same expiration dates, and same strike prices. The straddle writer expects "neutrality" or "lack of volatility". Stated another way, straddle writers are neither bullish nor bearish, but expect the underlying security to trade in a narrow range. Let us take a look at an example:

Eddie writes 1 GHI Nov 20 Straddle at 5. Eddie has two breakeven points:

Strike Price of call	+ Total Premium	= Upside Breakeven
20	+ 5	= $25

Strike Price of put	- Total Premium	= Downside Breakeven
20	+ 5	= $15

As a straddle writer, Eddie expects the stock to trade between $25 and $15 per share. Ideally, Eddie would like GHI stock to trade exactly at $20 per share at expiration. At $20, both options are at-the-money and would expire worthless.

25. **(C)**

Determining if an option is in-the-money or has intrinsic value differs for calls versus puts. A call option is in-the-money if the strike price is below the market price of the underlying security. A put option is in-the-money if the strike price is above the market price of the underlying security.

The Nov 20 puts (choice C) are in-the-money because the strike price is above the market value of Ford stock. The Aug 15 puts are out-of-the-money because the strike price is below the market value of Ford stock.

Choices A and D are out-of-the-money because the strike price of the call options are above the market value of Ford stock.

26. **(D)**

The question states that "Joan initiates a position". As a result, she would be opening a position. Since she initiates with a "purchase", this would be an "opening purchase". To liquidate her existing position, she would need to engage in a "closing sale". The two possibilities can be summarized as:

Initial Position is...	Liquidating Position is...
Opening Purchase	Closing Sale
Opening Sale	Closing Purchase

27. **(B)**

A preferred stock fund is sensitive to changes in interest rates, and behaves like a bond fund. Martin is concerned that interest rates will rise, and as a result, his fund will decline in value. So to best hedge his fund, he should purchase options that will increase in value if interest rates rise.

If interest rates rise, yield-based calls and interest rate put options will increase in value. Yield-based options are utilized to hedge or speculate on the direction of bond yields, while interest rate options are utilized to hedge or speculate on the direction of bond prices.

28. **(A)**

Gary has created a married put for tax purposes, meaning, when the stock and the put options are purchased on the same day, the cost basis of the stock and the put options are combined. Gary's purchase price of $50.75 on the stock plus the purchase of the puts for a premium of 3 are added together for a total cost basis of $53.75 per share. Gary's sales proceeds on the stock are $52, the price at which he actually sold the stock in the marketplace.

29. **(A)**

Kent has created a short combination, which consists of writing or selling a call(s) and a put(s) on the same security, but varying the expiration dates and/or strike prices. This is similar in concept to a short straddle in that the combination writer expects stability or neutrality. Stated another way, combination writers are neither bullish nor bearish, but expect the underlying security to trade in a narrow range.

30. **(A)**

The straddle writer is short both a call and a put on the same security, same expiration dates, and same strike prices. Since the investor is short 1 DEF June 65 put, he would need to write a call on the same security (DEF), same expiration date (June), and same strike price (65). Note that the premiums are not given in this question nor would the same premium be a requirement for a straddle.

Additionally, it is of importance to remember that a straddle writer assumes unlimited risk because a naked call option is embedded in the straddle writer's position. The writing of a straddle is only a suitable for investors that are willing to assume such risk.

31. **(D)**

Since the investor purchased the XDC Dec 105 calls for 3.14 and sold them for 2.11, he has generated a loss. The only two viable choices are B and D. To determine the dollar amount of the loss, utilize the following formula:

Premium (decimal moved two places to the left)	X number of contracts	X contract size	= Debit or Credit
.0314	X 10	X 10,000	-$3,140 debit
.0211	X 10	X 10,000	+$2,110 credit
= -$1,030 loss			

Note that on all foreign currency options tested on this exam, move the decimal point on the premium two places to the left. The contract size is also 10,000. The one exception is the Japanese Yen, in which the premium is moved four places to the left, and the contract size is 1 million.

32. **(A)**

A put option has intrinsic value if the strike price is above the market price of the underlying stock. Since the strike price is below the market price of DEF stock, the DEF May 55 Put option has zero intrinsic value. Note that there is no such concept as negative intrinsic value.

33. **(B)**

The position is a Protective Put Purchase, which consists of a long stock position and a long put. Taleen bought 1 GHI put option only as an insurance policy to protect against a decline in her long GHI stock position.

The breakeven point per share is the initial stock price plus the premium paid for the put. So, first we need to calculate the breakeven point. Taleen needs GHI stock to rise to $42/share to recoup the 2-point premium paid for the put. So, at $42/share, the following would result: Taleen's GHI stock which was purchased at $40/share is sold at $42/share resulting in a 2 point profit. The 2 point profit on the sale of the stock is offset against the 2-point premium paid for the put option. The result is the breakeven point.

A profit is generated when the stock trades higher than $42/share. At $43/share, Taleen makes a profit of 3 points on the stock. The puts expire is worthless, resulting in a loss of 2 points. Netting out the 3-point profit on the stock and the 2-point loss on the put results in an overall profit of 1-point.

34. **(B)**

Claudia has created a Credit Put Spread. By buying 3 XON Sept 60 Puts at 5 and writing 3 XON Sept 65 Puts at 8, she has a net credit of 3 points. In other words, Claudia received more money than has been paid out, establishing a net credit of 3 points. We can determine the breakeven point as follows:

Strike Price from dominant leg of spread (the put option with the higher premium)	Net Credit	= Breakeven Point
65	3	= 62

The breakeven is $62/share. At $62, the Sept 60 puts that Claudia purchased are worthless. The Sept 65 puts have 3 points of intrinsic value and would be exercised against Claudia, creating a 3-point loss, which would be offset by the net credit that Claudia received by establishing the spread. Therefore, if XON stock is trading at $62/share at expiration, Claudia does not make or lose money.

35. **(A)**

The investor has established a net debit spread. In other words, the put that he purchased cost more than the put that he sold, resulting in a net debit or cash outlay of 1 point. The investor would be required to deposit 100% of the net debit. The formula for determining the investor's net debit in dollar terms is as follows:

Net Debit	X number of spreads	X contract size	= $net debit
1	X 1	X 100	= $100

36. **(B)**

Expecting the Federal Reserve Board to tighten interest rates translates to rising interest rates. So, we now must determine which two option positions would benefit from rising interest rates.

An investor that goes long (buys) yield-based call options is speculating that the yield or interest rate is going to rise. He would also benefit from going short (selling or writing) yield-based put options. If yields or interest rates were to rise, the investor that wrote yield-based puts would benefit as the put options would expire worthless because the yield or interest rate would move further away from the strike price of the put options.

37. **(C)**

Position limits apply to options on the same side of the market, and are summarized as follows:

Bullish Side of Market	Bearish Side of Market
Long Calls	Short Calls
Short Puts	Long Puts

Position limits for DEF options are 100,000 contracts on either the bullish or bearish side of the market. Since the trader is long 60,000 DEF call options (bullish side), we need to determine which additional position is permissible. Choice A, the addition of 45,000 short puts (bullish side) added to the long position of 60,000 call options (bullish) side would exceed the position limit of 100,000. Choice B, the addition of 42,000 long calls (bullish side) added to the long position of 100,000 would also exceed the position limit of 100,000. Choice C is permissible as 65,000 long puts (bearish side) is within the position limits for DEF stock. Choice D is tricky as it is on the bearish side of the market, but 105,000 contracts by itself exceeds the limit on the bearish side of the market.

38. **(B)**

An option is composed only of intrinsic value (if any) at expiration. Nancy's call option is composed of intrinsic value because the strike price of 55 is below the underlying T-bond's yield of 5.85% at expiration. We take the 5.85% yield and divide by 10 which equates to 58.50. Her call options have 3.50 points of intrinsic value. We can then determine the profit as follows:

Intrinsic Value	-Premium	= Profit
$350	-$300	= $50

Nancy earns a $50 profit.

39. **(D)**

Tony is a straddle writer. He is short on calls and puts on the same security, same expiration dates, and same strike prices. The key concept is that embedded in the straddle writer's position is a naked or uncovered call option, the latter of which lends the position to unlimited risk. Theoretically, the underlying stock could rise to infinity. The call option would be exercised by the buyer. This means the straddle writer (Tony) would receive an assignment notice which would trigger the obligation to sell XYZ stock at the strike price. Since Tony does not own XYZ stock, he would first need to purchase XYZ stock in the market at an infinite price, and then sell XYZ stock at the strike price of $30/share.

Like the naked call writer, the straddle writer has unlimited risk, and is only suitable for investors willing to assume high risk.

40. **(A)**

Open interest refers to the number of outstanding contracts in a particular class or series. Open interest reflects only the total number of option contracts for a given option series that have been opened, but not yet closed out. Increased open interest suggests an increase in liquidity for an option series. As an option series gets closer to expiration, open interest declines as investors and speculators close out their existing option positions and roll them out to later expiration dates.

41. **(B)**

The order in which activities take place when opening an options account are the following:

1. RR determines suitability
2. ODD is sent to the customer
3. Account approval by an ROP
4. Execution of a trade

Therefore, the last step in the process is execution of the options trade.

42. **(D)**

The investor has created a short combination, which consists of writing or selling a call(s) and a put(s) on the same security, and varying the expiration dates and/or strikes. This is similar in concept to a short straddle in that the combination writer expects stability or neutrality. Stated another way, combination writers are neither bullish nor bearish, but expect the underlying security to trade in a narrow range.

43. **(A)**

The investor's position results in a net debit of 3 points. When both options expired worthless, the investor realized his maximum loss of the net debit. The net debit in dollar terms can be determined as follows:

Net Debit	X number of contacts	X contract size	= $ net debit
-3	X 5	X 100	= -$1,500

44. **(C)**

Janice wrote a DEF call option with a strike price of 55. As the writer of call option, she would like the option to expire as worthless. The option will expire as worthless or have zero intrinsic value if the underlying stock is at 55 or less at expiration, which translates to below or at its strike price (I and III). Above its strike price (II), the call option would have intrinsic value, and therefore would be beneficial for the call buyer to exercise the option.

45. **(A)**

Pam has established a long combination. The maximum loss is limited to the total debit. Pam paid a total of 7.50 points for the call and put. In dollars, this translates to $750, which can be determined as follows:

Total Debit	X number of combinations	X contract size	= $Total Debit
7.50	X 1	X 100	= $750

Alternatively, each purchase can be calculated separately to arrive at the same answer:

Debit of Put	X number of contracts	X contract size	= $Debit
3	X 1	X 100	= $300

Debit of Call	X number of contracts	X contract size	= $Debit
4.5	X 1	X 100	= $450

The $300 debit for the put and the $450 debit for the call equal a total debit of $750.

46. **(D)**

The first step in the process is being able to identify an odd stock split, which always ends in a ratio other than 1. Examples include 3 for 2, 4 for 3, and 5 for 2. In the case of a 3 for 2 stock split, each shareholder will receive 3 shares for every 2 shares that is owned.

Option contracts are also impacted in that the exercise price decreases while the number of shares per contract increases proportionally. Note the number of contracts remain unchanged. Let us review an example:

Tom owns 1 ABC May 90 call option. ABC Company announces a 3 for 2 stock split. Following the split, Tom will now own:

- 1 ABC May 60 call, however the contract size is now 150 shares. For every 2 shares that Tom owned, he receives 3 shares (3/2 x 100 shares = 150 shares). The exercise price of 60 is determined by multiplying 2/3 x 90.

Also note, the aggregate exercise price remains unchanged at $9,000.

47. **(A)**

Paul has written a combination, which means he is short both a call and a put on the same security, same expiration dates and different strike prices. A combination writer always has two breakeven points which can be calculated in the following manner:

Strike Price of call	+ Total Premium	= Upside Breakeven
60	+ 8	= $68

Strike Price of put	- Total Premium	= Downside Breakeven
65	-8	= $57

It is important to add that a combination writer expects "neutrality" or "lack of volatility". In other words, combination writers are neither bullish nor bearish, but expect the stock to trade in a narrow range. So, between now and expiration of the options, Paul expects XYZ stock to trade within the range of $68 and $57 per share. Stated another way, Paul does not expect XYZ stock to trade above $68 or below $57 per share.

48. **(D)**

The speculator anticipates that the dollar will weaken against the Euro. In other words, the speculator believes the Euro will strengthen. Since the speculator believes the Euro will strengthen or rise in value, he would want to take bullish positions on the Euro, buying calls and selling puts.

49. **(D)**

The relevant pieces of information used to answer this question are the value of Rodney's portfolio, the beta of his portfolio (measure of portfolio volatility relative to an index), and the current value of the index. We then utilize this information by applying the following two steps:

Step 1
Value of stock portfolio (SPX Index Value X 100)
$5,000,000 (1250 X 100)
$\frac{\$5,000,000}{125,000}$ = 40 contracts

Step 2
Number of contracts (in step #1) X Portfolio's Beta
40 X 1.20 = 48 contracts

50. **(C)**

A credit call spread can be created by going short or writing 1 ABC Oct 80 call, and going long (buying) 1 ABC Oct 85 call. While no premiums are given in the question, the call option with the lower strike price will have a higher premium given the same expiration dates. Since the ABC 80 has been written, and the ABC 85 call has been purchased, the investor would receive more money than has been paid out. As a result, the investor would be a "net seller" or establish a net credit spread.

OPTIONS EXAM 2

1. Amy buys 1 EBAY Jan 30 put at 3 and also buys 1 Jan 30 call at 3.50. What is Amy's margin requirement?

    (A) $650
    (B) $350
    (C) $300
    (D) $325

2. An investor expects the S&P 500 Index ("SPX") to trade in a narrow range over the next six months. Which of the following strategies would be consistent with his expectation of SPX?

    (A) Short Combinations
    (B) Long Straddles
    (C) Long Horizontal spreads
    (D) Long Vertical spreads

3. An investor buys 1 XYZ Oct 60 call at 3, and sells 1 XYZ Oct 65 call at 2. What is the investor's margin requirement?

    (A) $300
    (B) $100
    (C) $200
    (D) $500

4. All options advertisements must be submitted to FINRA:

    (A) 5 days prior to first use
    (B) 5 days after first use
    (C) 10 days prior to first use
    (D) 10 days after first use

5. Tim bought 2 ABC Mar 35 puts at 3. What is Tim's maximum potential gain?

    (A) Unlimited
    (B) $7,000
    (C) $3,200
    (D) $6,400

6. Which one of the following strategies entails unlimited risk?

    (A) Covered call writing
    (B) Buying stock
    (C) Writing a Straddle
    (D) Buying a Straddle

7. Why would an investor purchase a straddle? She:

    (A) expects volatility.
    (B) expects neutrality.
    (C) is bullish.
    (D) is bearish.

8. Brock bought 300 shares of MP at $26 and sold 3 MP Mar 30 calls at a premium of 5. What is Brock's maximum potential gain?

    (A) Unlimited
    (B) $2,700
    (C) $1,700
    (D) $900

9. Rick buys a POD Apr 30 call at 3. Which two of the following characteristics best describe this strategy?

    I.   Bullish
    II. Bearish
    III. Unlimited gain potential
    IV. Limited gain potential

    (A) I and III
    (B) I and IV
    (C) II and III
    (D) II and IV

10. Byron sold 2 AMZN 150 calls at 6 when AMZN stock was trading at $149/share. At what price does AMZN need to trade for Byron to breakeven?

    (A) 144
    (B) 138
    (C) 162
    (D) 156

11. An investor would like to be positioned for a sharp decline in QRS stock with the smallest cash deposit. As her registered rep, which of the following strategies would you recommend to her?

(A) Write calls
(B) Sell the stock short
(C) Buy puts
(D) Buy straddles

12. An investor buys a T-bond July 100 put at 2.17. At what price will the investor breakeven?

(A) 97.15
(B) 97.83
(C) 102.17
(D) 102.15

13. Barney Bucks has a $3 million stock portfolio that he expects to decline over the next three to six months. He would like to hedge his portfolio with the S&P 100 (OEX) 550 puts. His portfolio has a beta of .90 and the value of the OEX Index is 582. How many puts will he need to purchase to properly hedge his portfolio?

(A) 52
(B) 49
(C) 55
(D) 46

14. An option trade is placed on Friday, March 10th. On what date will settlement take place?

(A) March 13th
(B) March 11th
(C) March 17th
(D) March 15th

15. A customer of BET Brokerage writes an ABC July 50 call for 6 and an ABC July 50 put for 5. The call is repurchased for 7, and the put is repurchased for 5.75. What is the resulting profit or loss?

(A) $175 loss
(B) $175 profit
(C) $275 loss
(D) $100 profit

16. Eight months ago, a customer of Brokerage Advisors Inc purchased 500 shares of GOOG stock at $135. The stock is currently trading at $280, and the customer would like to purchase 5 GOOG Sept 250 puts for 5. What are the consequences of purchasing these put options?

I.   If the stock remains at or above $250/share the puts will expire worthless
II. He no longer has unlimited upside potential on the stock since the position is now hedged
III. His holding period on the stock will remain unchanged.
IV. His holding period on the stock will be terminated

(A) I and II
(B) I and IV
(C) II and III
(D) II and IV

17. A debit put spread can be created from which two of the following?

I.   Long 1 DEF Oct 40 put
II. Short 1 DEF Oct 40 put
III. Long 1 DEF Oct 45 put
IV. Short 1 DEF Oct 45 put

(A) I and III
(B) I and IV
(C) II and III
(D) II and IV

18. Sue goes long 1 XYZ May 40 put at 3 and 1 XYZ May 45 call at 4.5. What is Sue's maximum loss?

(A) $750
(B) Unlimited
(C) $450
(D) $300

19. Which one of the following exercise styles is applicable to foreign currency options?

(A) Capped style
(B) North American style
(C) American style
(D) European style

20. Murphy purchases 100 shares of ABC at $30, and three weeks later he buys an ABC Sept 25 put at 7. If Murphy decides to exercise the put and deliver the stock when ABC is trading at $22, what will be the resulting loss?

   (A) $500
   (B) $1,200
   (C) $400
   (D) $3,700

21. Mr. Thomas buys 100 shares of IBM at $130 and also writes 1 IBM Aug 135 call at 4. What is Mr. Thomas's maximum potential loss?

   (A) $12,600
   (B) $13,000
   (C) $13,100
   (D) $13,500

22. Which of the following methods is NOT considered fair and equitable in allocating an assignment notice by a broker-dealer to one of its customers?

   (A) Random selection
   (B) Largest position
   (C) Oldest position
   (D) Any method deemed fair and equitable

23. In a cash account, an investor owns 500 shares of IBM stock. He has just decided to write 5 IBM Oct 60 calls at 4. What is his motivation for writing the call options?

   (A) To go long against the box
   (B) To hedge against a decline in his IBM stock
   (C) To lock in his gain on the long IBM stock
   (D) To increase the rate of return on his long IBM stock

24. A customer places a market order to buy an HD Sept 45 call which is trading at 4.25 - 4.35. Shortly thereafter, he liquidates his position when the options are trading at 4.40 - 4.50. What is the customer's resulting profit?

   (A) $5 Profit
   (B) $25 Profit
   (C) $15 Profit
   (D) $10 Profit

25. Bobby buys 500 shares of GO at $60, and also purchases 5 GO Nov 50 puts at 1. His maximum potential loss will be realized if the underlying stock trades at which of the following prices?

   (A) $51
   (B) $59
   (C) $47
   (D) $60

26. A customer writes 1 PFE July 25 put at 3 when the market price of the stock is at $28. At expiration, the maximum potential loss is:

   (A) $2,800
   (B) $300
   (C) $2,200
   (D) $2,500

27. What is the maximum expiration of a regular or standard option?

   (A) Nine months
   (B) Six months
   (C) Thirty-nine months
   (D) Twelve months

28. A trader is long 55,000 ABC put options. 100,000 contracts is the position limit for ABC. Which one of the following additional positions would be permissible?

   (A) 65,000 long calls
   (B) 102,000 short puts
   (C) 55,000 short calls
   (D) 50,000 long puts

29. On which two of the following exchanges do listed options trade?

    I.   Chicago Board Options Exchange
    II. Philadelphia Stock Exchange
    III. Chicago Stock Exchange
    IV. Philadelphia Options Exchange

    (A) I and II
    (B) I and III
    (C) II and III
    (D) II and IV

30. Ian buys 200 shares of IBM stock at $145. He also goes long 2 IBM Sept 145 puts at 3. At what price would IBM need to trade for Ian to breakeven?

    (A) $142
    (B) $148
    (C) $139
    (D) $151

31. An investor buys 3 Euro Nov 130 calls for 2.15 and later sells the calls for 3.28. What is the resulting profit?

    (A) $113
    (B) $33,900
    (C) $11,300
    (D) $339

32. Which of the following activities takes place last when opening an options account?

    (A) Account approval by an ROP
    (B) Execution of a trade
    (C) RR signs the new account form
    (D) ODD is sent to the customer

33. A U.S. company will be importing croissants from a French company. Per its agreement, the U.S. company is required to make its payments in Euros. To hedge against its currency risk, the U.S. company should:

    (A) Write calls on the Euro
    (B) Write puts on the Euro
    (C) Buy calls on the Euro
    (D) Buy puts on the Euro

34. On February 8th, Mary buys 1 KLM July 55 put and writes I KLM Sept 60 put. Which two of the following correctly describe her position?

    I.   Debit spread
    II. Credit spread
    III. Horizontal spread
    IV. Diagonal spread

    (A) I and III
    (B) I and IV
    (C) II and III
    (D) II and IV

35. An investor writes 1 ABC July 35 call and simultaneously buys 1 ABC July 40 call. What is the name of this strategy?

    (A) Short Straddle
    (B) Short combination
    (C) Bearish diagonal call spread
    (D) Bearish vertical call spread

36. An investor sells short 1,000 ABC at $50, and also buys 10 ABC Sept 55 calls at 3. What is the investor's margin requirement?

    (A) $25,000
    (B) $28,000
    (C) $47,000
    (D) $53,000

37. A speculator initiates a position with the sale of 8 Nov 50 puts at 4. This is an example of:

    (A) a closing purchase
    (B) a closing sale
    (C) an opening sale
    (D) an opening purchase

38. Matt purchases an ABC Dec 60 call for $500 when the underlying stock is trading at $63. What is the intrinsic value of the call option?

    (A) $0
    (B) $300
    (C) $500
    (D) $200

39. Which two of the following are permissible methods a broker-dealer may use in allocating an assignment notice to one of its customers?

    I.   Largest position
    II. First-In, First-Out basis
    III. Smallest position
    IV. Random selection

    (A) I and II
    (B) I and III
    (C) II and III
    (D) II and IV

40. Ralph goes long 5 ABC Oct 65 calls and also goes long 5 ABC Oct 65 puts. What is Ralph's expectation of ABC stock? He:

    (A) expects volatility.
    (B) expects stability.
    (C) is bullish.
    (D) is bearish.

41. Ruth holds a security which gives her the right to sell a fixed number of shares of the underlying stock within the next 18 months. Which security does she hold?

    (A) LEAP
    (B) Call option
    (C) Warrant
    (D) Put option

42. Which one of the following is a correct statement regarding the adjustment of an options contract for an even stock split? The number of shares per contract is:

    (A) unchanged.
    (B) cancelled.
    (C) decreased.
    (D) increased.

43. In his options account, Mr. Brown writes 1 GHI Mar 85 put at 2. What is his maximum potential loss?

    (A) Unlimited
    (B) $8,300
    (C) $8,700
    (D) $8,500

44. Based upon events that are unfolding in the telecommunications industry, Leo expects VZ stock to trade in a very wide range over the next three to six months. Which one of the four option strategies will best allow Leo to capitalize on his expectation?

    (A) Short put
    (B) Horizontal call spread
    (C) Vertical call spread
    (D) Long straddle

45. Which two of the following are correct regarding options advertisements?

    I.   Must be approved by a GSP prior to use
    II. Must be approved by a ROP prior to use
    III. Must be filed with FINRA within ten days of first use
    IV. Must be filed with FINRA ten days prior to first use

    (A) I and III
    (B) I and IV
    (C) II and III
    (D) II and IV

46. Each customer that would like to engage in options trading must receive an Options Disclosure Document ("ODD') entitled the "Characteristics and Risks of Standardized Options". Within what time frame does the ODD need to be provided to each customer?

    (A) 15 days prior to account approval
    (B) Within 15 days of account approval
    (C) At or prior to the opening of the options account
    (D) No later than when the first trade is placed

47. An investor goes long 10 KO Sept 65 puts and goes short 10 KO Sept 70 puts. What is the investor's outlook for KO stock?

    (A) Stability
    (B) Volatility
    (C) Bullish
    (D) Bearish

48. Murat buys 100 HD at $45. He also goes long 1 Sept 40 Put at 2. At what price does HD stock need to trade for Murat to earn a profit?

    (A) $42
    (B) $47
    (C) $37
    (D) $48

49. All of the following are examples of broad-based index options EXCEPT:

    (A) Russell 2000 Index calls
    (B) S&P 500 Index puts
    (C) S&P Biotechnology Index calls
    (D) Nasdaq 100 Index puts

50. Which one of the following is a correct statement regarding the adjustment of an options strike price for a cash dividend? The number of contracts is:

    (A) decreased.
    (B) increased.
    (C) unchanged.
    (D) cancelled.

OPTIONS EXPLANATIONS 2

1. **(A)**

Amy has created a Long Straddle, which consists of the purchase of both a put and a call on the same security, strike prices, and expiration dates. The purchase of the put cost Amy $300 which is expressed as follows:

Premium	X number of contracts	X contract size	= $Premium
3	X 1	X 100	= $300

The purchase of the call cost Amy $350 which can be expressed as follows:

Premium	X number of contracts	X contract size	= $Premium
3.50	X 1	X 100	= $350

The Regulation T margin requirement is 100% of the purchase price of the put and the call. As a result, Amy must deposit $650.

2. **(A)**

Creating a Short Combination is consistent with his expectation of the SPX trading in a narrow range over the next six months. A Short Combination consists of writing or selling a call(s) and a put(s) on the same security with different expiration dates and/or strike prices. The Combination Writer expects stability or neutrality. In other words, the Combination writer is neither bullish nor bearish, but expects the underlying (index, security, or currency) to trade in a narrow range.

3. **(B)**

The investor has created a Net Debit Spread in that the purchase of the Oct 60 call exceeds the sale of the Oct 65 call. The investor's Regulation T margin requirement is 100% of the net debit, or $100 which can be expressed as follows:

Net Debit	X number of spreads	X contract size	= $Net Debit
1	X 1	X 100	= $100

4. **(C)**

An advertisement is any communication in which the broker-dealer cannot control the audience that is viewing, listening to, or watching the communication. Examples include: newspaper advertisements, commercials on radio and television.

Option Advertisements are of particular concern to FINRA in that they are a complex product, and the broker-dealer cannot control the audience that is viewing the communication. As a result, options advertisements are required to be submitted to FINRA's Advertising Regulations Department ten (10) days prior to first use.

5.   **(D)**

The purchase of a put(s) has limited gain potential. Tim is bearish as the put buyer, and can only profit from the strike price of 35 to zero, less the premium paid. If ABC stock falls to zero, Tim could purchase the stock at zero, and exercise his puts which would allow him to sell his stock at $35. Tim would then make a profit of 35 points less the 3 point premium. This can be expressed as follows:

Aggregate Exercise Price of put	-	$Premium	= $Profit (or loss)
$7,000	-	$600	=$6,400 profit

6.   **(C)**

A straddle writer assumes unlimited risk. The position consists of a Short Call and a Short Put on the same security with the same strike prices and expiration dates. Embedded in a Short Straddle is a Naked Call Option which lends the position to unlimited risk.

Writing a covered call involves limited risk. If the covered call writer receives an assignment notice, he is obligated to sell the underlying security at the exercise price. Since he owns the underlying security, he does not have to go to the market to make a purchase.

The naked put writer realizes his maximum loss upon assignment and he would be obligated to purchase the stock at the strike price. His maximum loss is the purchase price paid for the stock upon receiving an assignment notice less the premium received.

Long stock also has limited risk in that the maximum loss would be realized if the stock declined to zero.

7.   **(A)**

The Straddle Buyer is long both a call and a put on the same security, same expiration dates, and same strike prices. The Straddle Buyer expects "volatility" in the underlying security. In other words, the Straddle Buyer is neither bullish nor bearish, but expects the stock to fluctuate in a wide range. Let us take review an example:

Taleen buys 1 JKL Dec 20 straddle at 5 Taleen has two breakeven points: $25/share and $15/share which can be determined as follows:

Strike Price of Call Option	+ Total Premium	= Upside Breakeven Point
20	+ 5	= 25

Strike Price of Put Option	- Total Premium	= Downside Breakeven Point
20	- 5	= 15

As a Straddle Buyer, Taleen expects the stock to trade above $25 or $15. Taleen needs a large move in the stock either to the upside or downside to recoup the total premium paid for the call and the put.

8. **(B)**

Brock has created a covered call writing strategy. As a covered call writer, Brock is long stock and writes a call on the underlying stock. Let us take a closer look at Brock's position:

Bought 300 MP at $26
Sold 3 MP Mar 30 calls at 5

This is a conservative or low risk strategy, so Brock's profit will also be limited. Brock purchased the stock at $26, and cannot profit above $30 (strike price) plus the premium received. In other words, Brock can only profit up to $30 as the buyer of the call would exercise the option above $30 and Brock would be obligated to sell the stock at $30. He would be limited to a 4 point profit plus the 5 point premium received. In dollars, Brock's profit is limited to:

Transaction	Debit or Credit
Bought 300 MP at $26	-$7,800 debit
Sold 3 MP Mar 30 calls at 5	+$1,500 credit
Assignment of calls – obligation to sell 300 shares of MP at $30	+$9,000 credit
= $2,700 Profit	

9. **(A)**

Rick purchases a call which is a bullish position. Rick is positioned to profit from a rise in POD stock. Theoretically, POD stock could rise to infinity. Rick would then exercise his call option, purchasing POD stock at $30, and selling it in the market at an infinite price.

10. **(D)**

Byron breaks even when AMZN stock trades $156. The formula for determining the breakeven for a call option is as follows:

Strike Price	+ Premium	= Breakeven Point
150	+ 6	= 156

At $156, the buyer would exercise his call since it would have 6 points of intrinsic value. Byron would receive an assignment notice which would obligate him to sell the stock at $150. Since Byron does not own the stock, he would first need to go out to the market and purchase the stock at $156, realizing a 6 point loss. This 6 point loss would then be offset against the 6-point which was received. As a result, Byron would not make or lose any money.

11. **(C)**

Buying puts (long puts) would provide the greatest degree of leverage with the smallest cash deposit. The put buyer is positioned to profit from the strike price to zero, less the premium paid. The cash deposit would be limited to the premium paid.

Choice A, writing calls would limit the investor's profit to the premium received. Choice B, selling the stock short is also a viable strategy, however the cash deposit would be 50% of the sales proceeds which would exceed the premium paid for the put. Choice (D), Buy Straddles would require a greater cash outlay as the investor would be required to deposit the premium for the put and the call. Additionally, there would be no reason to purchase a call if the investor expected a sharp decline in QRS stock.

12.   **(A)**

The formula for determining the breakeven point on a put option is the following:

Strike Price	- Premium	= Breakeven Point

It is important to note, T-Bonds (and T-Notes) are quoted as a Percentage of Par Value + 32nds. So, the premium of 2.17 is 2% of par value + 17/32. Now, let us return to equation.

Strike Price of Put Option	- Premium	= Breakeven Point
100	- 2.17	= 97.15

Let us further examine how we arrived at the breakeven point of 97.15:

100.00
- 2.17

While we can subtract 2 from 100, we cannot subtract 17/32 from 00/32 as we need the numerator to be larger than the denominator. So, we first need to borrow 1 (or 32/32) from the 100. It is then rewritten as follows:

99.32
- 2.17
97.15

13.   **(D)**

The relevant pieces of information used to answer this question are the value of Barney's portfolio, the beta of his portfolio (measure of portfolio volatility relative to an index), and the current value of the index. We then take this information, and go through the following two steps:

Step 1
Value of stock portfolio (OEX Index Value X 100)
$\frac{\$3,000,000}{(582 \times 100)} = 51.55$

Step 2
Number of contracts (in step #1) X Portfolio's Beta
51.55 X .90 = 46 contracts

14.   **(A)**

Regular-way settlement for an options transaction is the trade date + one business day or T + 1. Friday, March 10th is the trade date or "T". The next business day is on Monday, March 13th, not on Saturday March, 11th as in Choice B.

15.   **(A)**

The customer writes a Straddle for a total premium of 11 or $1,100. The customer then liquidates his position by purchasing the Straddle and closing out his position for a total premium of 12.75 or $1,275. These transactions result in a loss of $175.

Transaction	Debit or Credit
Wrote 1 ABC July 50 Call	+$600 credit
Wrote 1 ABC July 50 Put	+$500 credit
Bought 1 ABC July 50 Call	-$700 debit
Bought 1 ABC July 50 Put	-$575 debit
Net Debit or loss = -$175	

16.   **(B)**

The position is a Protective Put Purchase, which means it consists of a long stock position and a long put(s). The investor is using the long puts as only an insurance policy to protect against a decline in his long stock position.

If the stock remains at or above $250/share, the GOOG put options will expire worthless. The GOOG put options will only be exercised if GOOG stock trades below $250/share and as a result, the put options go "in-the-money" or have intrinsic value.

The investor's holding period will be terminated by the purchase of put options within the first year (12 months). By purchasing the puts on GOOG, the investor terminates his holding period on the stock, since the GOOG puts eliminate the holder's downside risk on GOOG stock.

17.   **(C)**

A *debit put spread* can be established by purchasing (long) a put with *the higher strike price* (given that they have the same expiration dates) and writing or selling (short) with the lower strike price.

The put with the higher strike price would have a higher premium than the put option sold, resulting in a net debit. So, purchasing (long) 1 DEF Oct 45 put and writing (short) 1 DEF Oct 40 put would result in a debit put spread.

18.   **(A)**

Sue has purchased a Combination which consists of the purchase or sale of a put and a call, same security, different expiration dates and/or strike prices. Like the Straddle buyer, the Combination buyer expects volatility. Sue's maximum loss is limited to the total premium paid for the put and the call and her total premium is 7.5 or $750.

19.   **(D)**

Foreign currency options have a European-Style Exercise. A European-Style option can only be exercised at one specified period of time, usually the day prior to expiration. Even though foreign currency options have a European-Style Exercise, they still can be bought and sold each trading day on the Philadelphia stock exchange.

An American-Style option contract is one that may be exercised any time prior to its expiration date, allowing the holder maximum flexibility. All equity options are American-Style Exercise.

20. **(B)**

Murphy's purchases consist of $3,000 for the stock plus $700 for the put for a total cost of $3,700. Murphy exercises the put which gives him the right to sell the stock at the strike price of 25 ($2,500 in sales proceeds). Since Murphy had a purchase price of $3,700 and sales proceeds of $2,500, the resulting loss is $1,200. Note the fact that ABC stock is trading at $22 is irrelevant since Murphy did not sell the stock in the market at $22.

We arrive at the $1,200 loss as follows:

Transaction	Debit or Credit
Bought 100 ABC at $30	-$3,000 (debit)
Bought 1 ABC Sept 25 Put at 7	-$700 (debit)
Exercise of Sept 25 Put (right to sell at $25/share)	+$2,500 (credit)
-$1,200 debit or loss	

21. **(A)**

Writing a Covered Call involves limited risk. If the Covered Call Writer receives an assignment notice, he is obligated to sell the underlying security at the exercise price. Since he owns the underlying security, he does not have to go to the market to make a purchase.

This is a conservative strategy because the maximum loss is the amount paid for the stock minus the premium received for writing the option. Mr. Thomas would realize his maximum loss if the stock declined to zero. At zero, he would lose $13,000 on his stock purchase less the premium of $400 received. This results in a $12,600 loss. The maximum loss on a Covered Call Writing strategy can be summarized as follows:

Purchase Price Stock	-	Premium	= Maximum Loss
$13,000	-	$400	= $12,600

22. **(B)**

When a broker-dealer receives an assignment notice from the Options Clearing Corporation ("OCC"), it may allocate the assignment notice using any method deemed fair and equitable. Allocating an assignment notice based upon the largest position (or smallest position) is considered discriminatory, and not fair and equitable.

Random selection, oldest position (First-in-First-out), or any other method deemed fair and equitable are all acceptable methods for a broker-dealer allocating assignment notices.

23. **(D)**

The investor has created a Covered Call Writing strategy, which is designed to increase the rate of return on his long IBM stock. In other words, this is an income-generating strategy as the call options are written to generate income. This strategy is popular with dividend paying stocks; the investor receives dividend income from the underlying stock in addition to the premium income received for writing the call options.

24. **(A)**

In the first scenario, the HD Sept 45 call is trading at: 4.25 – 4.35. The 4.25 refers to the bid, as this is the price at which the market maker is willing to buy the option. The 4.35 refers to the ask price as this is the price at which the market maker is willing to sell the option. Since the customer is not a market maker, he would purchase the option at the higher of the two prices (ask price), and the sell the option at the lower of the two prices (bid price). Let us take a closer look at both scenarios:

Transaction	Trading	Price Bought or Sold	Debit or Credit
Bought 1 HD Sept 45 call	4.25 – 4.35	4.35	-$435 debit
Sold 1 HD Sept 45 put	4.40 – 4.50	4.40	+$440 credit
$5 profit			

25. **(C)**

The position is a Protective Put Purchase. A Protective Put Purchase consists of a long stock position and a long put(s). Bobby is using the long puts only as an insurance policy to protect against a decline in his long stock position.

Bobby's maximum loss will be realized when the underlying stock trades $50 or lower. At $47, Bobby would sell his 500 shares of GO stock at $50, not $47. This would be accomplished by exercising his put options and selling his 500 shares of GO at the strike price of $50. His maximum loss would be the following: the difference between the price in which he purchased the stock ($60) and the sale price of the stock through exercising the puts ($50) + the 1 point premium paid for the put. This totals an 11 point loss x 500 shares of stock = -$5,500.

26. **(C)**

The Put Writer is bullish, as he could receive an assignment notice, and therefore be obligated to purchase the stock at the strike price. His maximum potential loss would be the price he was assigned the stock less the premium received. The put writer's maximum loss in dollars can be determined by using the following formula:

Aggregate Exercise Price	-	Premium	= Maximum Loss
$2,500	-	300	= $2,200

27. **(A)**

When a standard or regular option is initially issued by the Options Clearing Corporation ("OCC"), the initial expiration is nine (9) months.

Any listed option that exceeds nine (9) months expiration are called LEAPS (**L**ong-**T**erm **A**ntici**P**ation **S**ecurities). LEAPS are initially issued with 39-month expiration dates, and have January expiration dates.

28. **(A)**

Position limits apply to option positions on the same side of the market which can be summarized as follows:

Bullish Side of Market	Bearish Side of Market
Long ABC call options	Long ABC put options
Short ABC put options	Short ABC call options

Position limits for ABC options are 100,000 contracts on either the bullish or bearish side of the market.

Since the trader is long 55,000 ABC put options (bearish), we need to determine which additional position is permissible. Choice A, the addition of 65,000 long calls (bullish side) would be permissible since neither the bullish nor bearish side of the market exceeds position limits. Choice B would exceed the position limit as the short put (bullish) would total 102,000 contracts by itself. Choice C, which is the addition of 55,000 short calls (bearish) added to the long position of 55,000 puts would total 110,000 contracts on the bearish side, exceeding position limits. Choice D, 50,000 long puts (bearish) added to the existing long put position of 55,000 contracts (bearish) would total 105,000 contracts, exceeding the position limit.

29. **(A)**

Listed options trade on the Chicago Board Options Exchange ("CBOE") and the Philadelphia Stock Exchange ("Philx"). The Chicago Stock Exchange is a regional exchange that trades equity securities, not listed options. The Philadelphia Options Exchange does not exist, but appears to be a logical choice.

30. **(B)**

The position is a Protective Put Purchase that consists of a long stock position and a long put(s). Ian is long and the 2 IBM puts only as an insurance policy to protect against a decline in his long IBM stock position.

The breakeven point for a Protective Put Purchase can be expressed as follows:

Purchase Price of Stock	+ Premium	= Breakeven Point
$145/share	+ 3	= $148/share

So, at $148/share, the following would result: Ian's IBM stock which was purchased at $145/share is sold at $148/share resulting in a 3 point profit. The 3-point profit on the sale of the stock is offset against the 3-point premium paid for the put options. The result is no gain or loss.

31. **(D)**

The customer has earned a profit of $339. The purchase of 3 Euro Nov 130 calls at a premium of 2.15 which translates to $645. We arrive at $645 by utilizing the following method:

For all foreign currencies on the Series 7 exam with one exception, the contract size is 10,000. The one exception is the Japanese Yen, wherein you move the decimal on the premium two places to the left. So, the premium is rewritten as .0215. Now the following formula can be applied:

Premium	X Contract Size	X Number of Contracts	= $Premium
.0215	X 10,000	X 3	= $645

The three Euro contracts are then sold for 3.28 which translates to:

Premium	X Contract Size	X Number of Contracts	= $Premium
.0328	X 10,000	X 3	= $984

Now it is just a matter of simple subtraction:

Sales Price	-	Purchase Price	= Profit (or loss)
$984	-	$645	= $339

32. **(B)**

The first two steps that take place when opening an options account are the RR signing the new account form and the Options Disclosure Document ("ODD") being sent to the customer. Note, the order of these two steps may vary or may even be simultaneous. However, the principal will not approval the account until both of these steps have taken place. It is only after the Registered Options Principal ("ROP") approves the account will a customer order be accepted for execution.

33. **(C)**

The U.S. company is concerned about currency risk. However, the question does not state if the U.S. company is concerned with a rising or falling Euro against the U.S. dollar. As an importer that will be paying in Euros, the fear or risk is that the Euro will rise. When it is time to exchange U.S. dollars for Euros, the U.S. dollars will purchase less Euros. Effectively, this will increase the company's cost of the croissants. To hedge against a rise in the Euro, the U.S. company should buy calls on the Euro, which is a bullish position. So, if the Euro does rise against the dollar, any loss in the foreign exchange market would be offset against an increase in value in the Euro options.

Choice B, while a bullish position on the Euro, would limit the maximum gain to the premium received for writing the puts. Choices A and D are bearish positions on the Euro, and therefore on the wrong side of the market.

34.   **(D)**

The first step is being able to identify that this is a Credit Spread.

While no premiums were given in the question, you are able to determine which option has a higher premium. The option with the longer expiration date (Sept) and the put option with the higher strike price, if instead these were call options, would be the call option with the lower strike price. Both of these factors attribute to a higher premium for the KLM Sept 60 put. The investor writes or sells the 60 put, which brings in more money that is paid out for the 55 put. As a result, the investor is a "net seller" or has established a Credit Spread.

This is also a Diagonal Spread as it consists of the purchase and sale of both puts (or calls) on the same security with different expiration dates and strike prices.

35.   **(D)**

This is a Bearish Vertical Call Spread. Let us review the steps to determine how we arrived at this:

- A spread involves a purchase and sale; one option was written and the other was purchased;
- The investor is Bearish; the focus is on the dominant leg of the spread; this is the more valuable option. The call option with the lower strike price is more valuable or would have a higher premium (given the same expiration date of July).

36.   **(B)**

This strategy is a Protective Call Purchase. The investor has sold ABC stock short and purchases call options as an insurance policy (hedge) to protect against a rise in ABC stock. The Regulation T margin requirement is 50% of the short sale or $25,000 plus 100% of the premium or $3,000. The total is $28,000.

37.   **(C)**

The question states that the speculator "initiates a position". As a result, he would be opening a position. Since he initiates with a "sale", this would be an "opening sale". To liquidate his existing position, he would need to engage in a "closing purchase". The two possibilities can be summarized as:

Initial Position is …	Liquidating Position is …
Opening Purchase	Closing Sale
Opening Sale	Closing Purchase

38.   **(B)**

The intrinsic value or in-the-money value for a call option can be determined by focusing on the relationship between the strike price and the market price of the underlying stock. A call option has intrinsic value or is in-the-money when strike price or exercise price is below the market price of the stock. With a strike price of 60 and a market price of $63, the calls have 3 points or $300 of intrinsic value. We can summarize the relationship of intrinsic value for calls and puts below:

Intrinsic Value for a Call Option	Intrinsic Value for a Put Option
Strike Price is below the market price of the underlying security	Strike Price is above the market price of the underlying security

39.   **(D)**

A broker-dealer may utilize a First-in, First-Out method or Random Selection when allocating an assignment notice to a customer.

Largest Position and Smallest Position are considered discriminatory and are therefore not permissible. The method of exercise and assignment differs for a broker-dealer versus the Options Clearing Corporation ("OCC"), as summarized below:

Broker-Dealer may allocate an assignment notice to one of its customers based upon…	The OCC may allocate an assignment notice to a broker-dealer based upon…
<ul><li>First-in-, First-Out Method</li><li>Random Selection</li></ul>	<ul><li>Random Selection</li></ul>

40.   **(A)**

You should be able to identify the position as a long Straddle. The Straddle buyer is long both a call and a put on the same security, same expiration dates, and same strike prices. The Straddle buyer expects "volatility" in the underlying security. Stated another way, Straddle buyers are neither bullish nor bearish, but expect the stock to fluctuate in a wide range. Let us now take a closer look at Ralph's position, and let us add a premium to our example to illustrate this:

Ralph buys 5 ABC Oct 65 straddles at 7.
Ralph has two breakeven points:

Strike Price of Call Option	+ Total Premium	= Upside Breakeven Point
65	+ 7	= 72

Strike Price of Put Option	- Total Premium	= Downside Breakeven Point
65	- 7	= 58

As a straddle buyer, Ralph expects the stock to trade above $72 or below $58. He needs a large move in the stock either to the upside or downside to recoup the total premium paid for the call and put.

41.   **(A)**

Ruth is holding a LEAP or **L**ong -**T**erm **E**quity **A**ntici**P**ation of **S**ecurities. Standard or regular options have a maximum expiration date of 9-months when issued. LEAPS on the other hand, have a maximum expiration date of up to 39-months. LEAPS also give the holder either the right to buy or sell the underlying security just like a standard call or put option.

We can eliminate Choices B and D as the maximum expiration for a standard call or put option cannot exceed nine months. A Warrant (Choice C) can be perpetual or long-term in nature, but only give the holder the right to buy the underlying security. Therefore, Choice C can be eliminated.

42.   **(A)**

Option contracts are adjusted for even splits as follows:

- The number of contracts increases;
- The strike price decreases proportionally

However, the number of shares per contract remains fixed at 100.

43. **(B)**

The Put Writer is bullish, as he could receive an assignment notice, and therefore be obligated to purchase the stock at the strike price. His maximum potential loss would be the price he was assigned the stock less the premium received. The put writer's maximum loss in dollars can be determined by using the following formula:

Aggregate Exercise Price	- Premium	= Maximum Loss
$8,500	- 200	$8,300 loss

44. **(D)**

A Long Straddle consists of buying both a call and a put on the same security, same expiration dates, and same strike prices. The straddle buyer expects "volatility" in the underlying security. Stated another way, straddle buyers are neither bullish nor bearish, but expect the stock to fluctuate in a wide range. Let's take a look at an example:

Leo buys 1 VZ Sept 40 straddle at 7
Leo has two breakeven points:

Strike Price of Call Option	+ Total Premium	= Upside Breakeven Point
40	+ 7	= 40

Strike Price of Put Option	- Total Premium	= Downside Breakeven Point
40	- 7	= 33

As a straddle buyer, Leo expects the stock to trade above $40 or below $33. He needs a large move in the stock either to the upside or downside to recoup the total premium paid for the call and put options.

45. **(D)**

Options advertisements must be approved by Registered Options Principal ("ROP") (Series 4) prior to use. A General Securities Principal ("GSP") (Series 24) may not approve options advertisements unless he or she is also an ROP and holds the Series 4 license. All options advertisements must be filed with FINRA ten days prior to first use.

46. **(C)**

Each customer that would like to engage in options trading must receive the Options Disclosure Document ("ODD") at or prior to the opening of the options account. In other words, it is acceptable to send the ODD to the customer in advance of opening the account, but no later than the time the account is being opened.

The ROP (Series 4) will not approve the account for options trading unless the customer is suitable for options trading and has also received the ODD.

47.   **(C)**

The investor has created a Bullish Spread. While no premiums are given in the question, the put option with the higher strike price (given the same expiration dates) would have the higher premium. This is because it would give the holder of the put the right to sell KO stock at 70 versus the 65 put which would give the holder the right to sell the stock at 65.

Once we have determined that the KO Sept 70 puts have the higher premium, we can now focus on this option series. Since the investor is short or selling the KO Sept 70 Puts, he is bullish. The investor potentially has an obligation to buy KO stock at 70, and therefore may acquire a long position in KO stock at $70.

48.   **(D)**

The position is a Protective Put Purchase, which consists of a long stock position and a long put. Murat bought 1 HD put option only as an insurance policy to protect against a decline in his long HD stock position.

The breakeven point per share is the initial stock price plus the premium paid for the put. So, first we need to determine the breakeven point. Murat needs HD stock to rise to $47 to recoup the 2-point premium paid for the put. So, at $47, Murat's HD stock, which was purchased at $45, is sold at $47, resulting in a 2-point profit. The 2-point profit on the sale of the stock is offset against the 2-point premium paid for the put option. The result is the breakeven point.

A profit is generated when the stock trades higher than $47. At $48, Murat earns a profit of 3 points on the stock. The puts expire worthless, resulting in a loss of 2 points. Netting out the 3-point profit on the stock against the 3-point loss on the put results in an overall profit of 1 point.

49.   **(C)**

The S&P Biotechnology Index calls are an example of a narrow-based Index option. This is because the index is limited to one industry or sector of the market. These index options tend to have more volatility as they are not diversified across industry lines as are broad-based index options. The Russell 2000, S&P 500, and the Nasdaq 100 Indices are diversified across industry lines and therefore broad-based indices.

50.   **(C)**

The number of contracts is not adjusted for cash dividends.
It is important to note that adjustments to the strike price of an option contract are made for stock dividends, even stock splits, and odd stock splits.

OPTIONS EXAM 3

1. An investor writes 10 ABC Nov 45 puts at 3. One month later, the investor receives an assignment notice when the stock is trading at $41. What is the investor's required cash deposit?

    (A) $45,000
    (B) $42,000
    (C) $41,000
    (D) $38,000

2. Which two of the following are True statements?

    I.   Vertical Debit Put Spreads are bullish.
    II. Vertical Debit Put Spreads are bearish
    III. Vertical Credit Call Spreads are bullish
    IV. Vertical Credit Call Spreads are bearish

    (A) I and III
    (B) I and IV
    (C) II and III
    (D) II and IV

3. Which of the following is a Bear Spread?

    (A) Long a Sept 60 call and short a Mar 65 call
    (B) Long a Sept 65 call and long a Mar 65 call
    (C) Short a Sept 65 call and long a Sept 70 call
    (D) Long a Sept 65 call and short a Sept 70 call

4. Which of the following is a correct statement regarding the purchase of a put option?

    (A) The buyer expects the stock to increase
    (B) The buyer would exercise the put if the stock price is higher than the strike price
    (C) It may be used to protect a long stock position
    (D) It may be used to increase the overall rate of return on a portfolio

5. Stuart buys 100 shares of DO at $35 and also buys a DO Dec 35 put at 5. Following these purchases, bad news is announced and DO stock declines to $22. Stuart reacts to this by exercising his put option. What is Stuart's resulting profit or loss?

    (A) $1,300 loss
    (B) $500 loss
    (C) $800 loss
    (D) $1,800 loss

6. Evan buys 1 QRS June 45 put and also buys 1 QRS Sept 45 call. What is this strategy called?

    (A) Combination
    (B) Horizontal spread
    (C) Hedge
    (D) Straddle

7. George buys 1 XDB (British Pound) June 155 call for 3.25. What is George's aggregate exercise price?

    (A) $15,825
    (B) $15,500
    (C) $1,875
    (D) $1,550

8. According to Regulation T, when is an investor required to pay for the purchase of an option contract?

    (A) Within two business days following the settlement date.
    (B) Within four business days following the settlement date.
    (C) Within one business day following the settlement date.
    (D) No later than the settlement date.

9. An investor buys an SPX (S&P 500) Sept 1245 index call for 7. At expiration, the index settles at 1235. As a result, the buyer would be obligated to pay the writer:

(A) $0
(B) $1,000
(C) $300
(D) $1,700

10. The Russell 2000 Index (RUT) is currently trading at 805. Which one of the following RUT options is in-the-money?

(A) Aug 805 puts
(B) Aug 800 calls
(C) Nov 810 calls
(D) Nov 800 puts

11. In his margin account, an investor purchases 3 ABC Mar 50 calls at 3. How much is the investor required to deposit?

(A) $450
(B) $900
(C) $150
(D) $300

12. An investor purchases a T-Bond Mar 95 Call at 2.17. This translates to a purchase price of:

(A) $253.125
(B) $2,531.25
(C) $217
(D) $2,170

13. If interest rates decline, what affect will that have on T-bond option premiums? Premiums on T-bond:

I. calls will increase
II. calls will decrease
III. puts will increase
IV. puts will decrease

(A) I and III
(B) I and IV
(C) II and III
(D) II and IV

14. Randy writes 5 Euro May 130 puts at 4. How can this strategy be characterized:

I. Bearish
II. Bullish
III. Limited loss potential
IV. Unlimited loss potential

(A) I and III
(B) I and IV
(C) II and III
(D) II and IV

15. Pam is short 1 AMZN Apr 40 put at 5 and also short 1 Apr 40 call at 4.75. At what prices will Pam break even?

I. 35
II. 44.75
III. 49.75
IV. 30.25

(A) I and II
(B) I and III
(C) II and III
(D) III and IV

16. The CBOE trades equity options each day until:

(A) 3:00pm CT
(B) 3:15pm CT
(C) 4:30pm CT
(D) 11:59pm CT

17. An investor is long an MNO May 45 put at 5 and is short an MNO Aug 50 put at 8. Which two of the following best describe this strategy?

I. Bearish
II. Bullish
III. Diagonal spread
IV. Horizontal spread

(A) I and III
(B) I and IV
(C) II and III
(D) II and IV

18. Gracie sells short 1,000 POP at $55 per share. She also buys 10 POP Sept 60 calls at 3. What is Gracie's breakeven point?

    (A) $63
    (B) $57
    (C) $52
    (D) $58

19. Ted writes 1 NGT Dec 30 call at 3.25, and also writes 1 NGT Dec 30 put at 3. At expiration, at what price would the underlying stock need to trade for Ted to achieve his maximum gain?

    (A) $27
    (B) $36.25
    (C) $30
    (D) $33.25

20. Marissa sells short 1,000 ROZ at $55 per share. She also buys 10 ROZ Oct 60 calls at 3. What is Marissa's maximum loss?

    (A) $8,000
    (B) $3,000
    (C) Unlimited
    (D) $52,000

21. William writes 2 XYZ Jan 80 calls at a premium of 2. At which price does William break even?

    (A) $78
    (B) $76
    (C) $82
    (D) $84

22. Josh goes long 1 XYZ Oct 35 put at 6. What is his maximum potential loss?

    (A) $3,500
    (B) $600
    (C) Unlimited
    (D) $4,100

23. All of the following features of an options contract are determined by the exchanges where options trade EXCEPT:

    (A) Strike Price
    (B) Contract Size
    (C) Expiration Date
    (D) Premium

24. Which two of the following are bullish spreads?

    I.   Net debit vertical call spread
    II. Net credit vertical call spread
    III. Net debit vertical put spread
    IV. Net credit vertical put spread

    (A) I and III
    (B) I and IV
    (C) II and III
    (D) II and IV

25. Mr. Walck writes 1 PQR July 75 call 3. What is his maximum loss?

    (A) The aggregate exercise + premium
    (B) The aggregate exercise price - premium
    (C) Premium
    (D) Unlimited

26. The AMZN Sept 140 put would be in-the-money if the underlying stock was trading at which of the following prices?

    (A) 141.75
    (B) 145
    (C) 140
    (D) 138.25

27. Gary buys a Swiss Franc June 100 put option for a premium of 2.55. At what price would the Swiss Franc need to trade for Gary to breakeven?

    (A) 102.55
    (B) 100.02
    (C) 99.97
    (D) 97.45

28. Which one of the following has unlimited gain potential?

    (A) Long call
    (B) Short call
    (C) Long put
    (D) Short put

29. A customer expects XOM stock to trade in a narrow range over the next six to nine months. He would like to implement a strategy to generate maximum income that is also consistent with his outlook for the stock. As his RR, which of the following would you recommend?

    (A) Write calls
    (B) Write Straddles
    (C) Write spreads
    (D) Write puts

30. An investor created the following position:

    Long 1 MSFT Dec 25 call
    Short 1 MSFT Dec 30 call

    Which two characteristics are TRUE of this position?

    I.   Debit
    II. Credit
    III. Bullish
    IV   Bearish

    (A) I and III
    (B) I and IV
    (C) II and III
    (D) II and IV

31. Patricia writes 3 AMZN July 150 puts at 5. Three days later, the puts are liquidated at 5.50. What is the resulting profit or loss?

    (A) $150 profit
    (B) $150 loss
    (C) $50 profit
    (D) $50 loss

32. Mr. Duffy bought 3 MNO Feb 75 puts at 3. Where does the underlying stock need to trade for Mr. Duffy to breakeven?

    (A) $78
    (B) $72
    (C) $84
    (D) $66

33. Ryan writes 1 XDN (Japanese Yen) Aug 120 put. Four months later, he receives an assignment notice. What is Ryan's aggregate cost upon assignment?

    (A) $1,200
    (B) $12,000
    (C) $120
    (D) $120,000

34. Which one of the following strategies entails unlimited risk?

    (A) Short stock and long call
    (B) Short stock and short put
    (C) Long stock and short call
    (D) Long stock and short put

35. A client buys two June 35 calls on Baker Industries at 3. What is the client's cost basis?

    (A) $6,000
    (B) $3,000
    (C) $600
    (D) $300

36. According to industry regulations, when is an investor required to pay for the purchase of a put option?

    (A) T + 2
    (B) T + 1
    (C) T + 5
    (D) T + 3

37. Seymour writes 5 XON Oct 75 calls at a premium of 7. With the stock trading at $77 per share, how much time value do Seymour's call options have?

    (A) 7 points
    (B) 0 points
    (C) 2 points
    (D) 5 points

38. A long call can be utilized to protect which of the following positions?

    (A) Long stock position
    (B) Short stock position
    (C) Long put position
    (D) Short put position

39. If interest rates decline, what affect will that have on yield-based option premiums? Premiums on yield-based:

    I.   calls will increase
    II. calls will decrease
    III. puts will increase
    IV. puts will decrease

    (A) I and III
    (B) I and IV
    (C) II and III
    (D) II and IV

40. CBOE Gold Index options cease trading each day at:

    (A) 4:15pm eastern time
    (B) 4:00pm eastern time
    (C) 11:59pm eastern time
    (D) 5:30pm eastern time

41. An investor writes a T-Bond put option for a premium of 3.14. This investor will receive:

    (A) $3,437.50
    (B) $343.75
    (C) $3,140
    (D) $314

42. Scott goes long 2 MNO Nov 55 puts at 3. What is his maximum potential loss?

    (A) $300
    (B) $600
    (C) $11,600
    (D) Unlimited

43. Which two of the following strategies has unlimited loss potential?

    I.   Short stock position
    II. Writing uncovered calls
    III. Writing covered calls
    IV. Long stock position

    (A) I and II
    (B) I and III
    (C) II and III
    (D) II and IV

44. An investor sells short 1,000 DEF at $40 and also writes 10 DEF July 40 puts at 5. What is the investor's margin requirement?

    (A) $40,000
    (B) $35,000
    (C) $15,000
    (D) $20,000

45. An investor exercises an IBM June 50 call that was purchased at a premium of 3. What is the investor's cost basis on the stock?

    (A) $4,700
    (B) $5,000
    (C) $5,000
    (D) $5,300

46. An investor initiates a position by writing 5 JTU Apr 65 calls at 3. Which two of the following would be the correct method of marking the options order ticket?

    I. Closing sale
    II. Opening sale
    III. Covered
    IV. Uncovered

    (A) I and III
    (B) I and IV
    (C) II and III
    (D) II and IV

47. Which of the following securities does Not give the holder the right to buy the underlying stock?

    (A) Warrant
    (B) Put option
    (C) Call option
    (D) Right

48. Which one of the following methods does the Options Clearing Corporation utilize when allocating an assignment notice to a broker-dealer?

    (A) Largest position
    (B) Smallest position
    (C) Random selection basis
    (D) First-in, first-out basis

49. Atwood writes 3 XON May 75 calls at a premium of 3. At what price does the underlying stock need to trade for Atwood to breakeven?

    (A) $72
    (B) $78
    (C) $60
    (D) $90

50. Which strategy has unlimited loss potential?

    (A) Short Swiss Franc put option
    (B) Long Euro call option
    (C) Short Yen call option
    (D) Long British Pound put

OPTIONS EXPLANATIONS 3

1.   **(B)**

The investor received an assignment notice which obligates him to buy 1,000 shares (10 contracts) of ABC stock at the exercise price of $45/share for a total of $45,000. Since the investor initially received a $3,000 credit for writing the puts, he is required to deposit an additional $42,000 since he already has a $3,000 credit in his account.

In other words, when the question asks for the "cash deposit", the correct approach is the aggregate exercise price less the premium received. However, if the question asked for the "required margin" or the "Regulation T deposit", the answer would be $45,000.

2.   **(D)**

Vertical Debit Put Spreads are a bearish strategy. Here is an example:

Transaction	Debit or Credit
Buy 1 XYZ Dec 60 Put	= 5 debit
Sell 1 XYZ Dec 55 Put	= 3 credit
Net Debit = 2	

The Dec 60 put has a larger premium because the put with the higher strike price is more valuable, given the same expiration dates. In determining the investor's expectation, we focus on the leg of the spread with the higher premium. Since the investor is the buyer of the Dec 60 Put (bearish), we can determine that the investor is bearish.

Vertical Credit Call Spreads are Bearish. Here is an example:

Transaction	Debit or Credit
Buy 1 XYZ Dec 60 Call	= 3 debit
Sell 1 XYZ Dec 55 Call	= 5 credit
Net Credit = 2	

The Dec 55 call has a larger premium because the call with the lower strike price is more valuable, given the same expiration dates. In determining the investor's expectation, we focus on the leg of the spread with the higher premium. Since the investor is the seller of the Dec 55 Call (bearish), we can determine that the investor is bearish.

3.   **(C)**

This question tests your understanding of which factors attribute to a higher versus a lower premium for a call option. The two factors which attribute to a higher premium are:

- Call option with the lower strike price
  A 60 call would have a higher premium than a 65 call, and a 65 call would have a higher premium than a 70 call. The lower strike price would give the buyer of the call the right to purchase the stock at the lower strike price.

- The longer expiration date
  The longer expiration date has greater time value. So, it is important to understand that Sept options would have a higher premium given the greater time value. So, the September options would have a higher premium than the March options. Some of you reading this explanation may argue that this depends on the date in which you are looking at these options. While this is correct, the exam will assume that if you are not given a date, assume you are early in the year. So, if you are looking at these options in the month of January, September would be more value as it has the greater time value.

Choice C – Short Sept 65 call would have a higher premium than the 70 call. In determining the investor's expectation, we focus on the leg of the spread with the higher premium. Since the investor is short (writer) Sept 65 call (bearish), we can determine that the investor is bearish.

4. **(C)**

An investor may purchase a put option to either speculate or protect (hedge) an existing position. Here is an example of a Protective Put Purchase:

Transaction	Outlook
Long 1,000 XYZ at $50	Bullish
Long 10 XYZ Oct 45 puts at 3	Bearish

The investor is bullish since he has more money invested in the long stock position. The puts are purchased only as an insurance policy. If XYZ stock were to decline sharply, the investor would be able to exercise his puts, giving him the right to sell his stock at $45.

5. **(B)**

Stuart has created a Protective Put Purchase. He purchased 100 shares of DO stock at $35. Since the stock declined sharply ($22/share), he decides to exercise his puts which allows him to sell his stock at $35 (exercise price). Stuart's only loss is the $500 premium paid for the put option. This can be expressed as follows:

Transaction	Debit or Credit
Bought 100 DO at $35	-$3,500 debit
Bought 1 DO Dec 35 Put @ 5	-$500 debit
Exercise of Put – Right to sell stock 100 shares at $35	+$3,500 credit
-$500 loss	

6. **(A)**

This strategy is called a Combination, which consists of the purchase or sale of a put and a call, same security, different expiration dates and/or strike prices. Like the Straddle Buyer, the Combination buyer also expects volatility.

7.　　**(B)**

George's aggregate or total exercise price is $15,500. The premiums are not taken into consideration when determining the aggregate exercise price. When George exercises his call, he is exchanging $15,500 for 10,000 British pounds. This can be summarized as follows:

Strike Price (move decimal point on the premium two places to the left)	X Contract Size	X number of contracts	= Aggregate Exercise Price
1.55	X 10,000	X 1	= $15,500

8.　　**(B)**

The Regulation T payment date is the trade date plus five business days or T + 5. Since options are required to settle within one business day following the trade date or T + 1, "within four days following the settlement date" would be equal to T + 5. In other words, T + 1 plus an additional 4 business days equals T + 5.

9.　　**(A)**

This is a trick question. The buyer is never obligated to pay the writer. The buyer's maximum loss is limited to the premium paid. On the other hand, if the option has intrinsic value at expiration, the writer is obligated to pay the buyer the in-the-money amount at expiration. Note, this is only true in the case of cash-settled options.

10.　　**(B)**

Call options are in-the-money or have intrinsic value when the exercise price is below the market price. With the exercise price at 800 and the market price at 805, the Aug 800 calls are in-the-money. Put options are in-the-money or have intrinsic value when the exercise price is above the market price.

11.　　**(B)**

The Regulation T margin requirement for the purchase of an option(s) is 100%, regardless of whether this is purchased in a margin account or a cash account. The premium of $900 can be determined as follows:

Premium	X Number of Contracts	X Contract Size	= Total Premium
3	3	100	= $900

12.　　**(B)**

The premium equates to a purchase price of $2,531.25. To determine the premium, you will need to know the following:

- T-Bond (T-Note) options are quoted as a percentage of par value + 32nds
- Par value or the contract size is $100,000
- The value of 1/32 is equal to $31.25 ($1,000/32 = $31.25)

Now, we can determine the premium as follows:

Premium		X number of contracts	= $Total Premium
2.17			
(2% x par value)	+ 17/32		
(2% x $100,000)	+ 17 X $31.25		
$2,000	+ $531.25		
$2,531.25		X 1	= $2,531.25

13.   **(B)**

The fundamental concepts of bonds apply to both the underlying Treasury Bonds and T-Bond Options. Both T-bonds and T-bond options have an inverse relationship to interest rates. If interest rates decline, T-bond prices rise. Since T-bond options are price based, if T-bonds rise in price, T-bond call premiums rise and T-bond put premiums decline.

The relationship between the underlying security the premium of calls and puts are the same as they are for equity options, and is summarized below.

Relationship	Call Premium	Put Premium
If the underlying security were to increase...	Increase	Decline
If the underlying security were to decline...	Decline	Increase

14.   **(C)**

This strategy can be characterized as bullish and entails limited risk. Regardless of whether this is an equity option, interest rate option, or currency option, the same concepts apply. That is:

- Writing puts is a bullish strategy as the writer may be obligated to purchase the underlying security or currency at the exercise price. Since the writer would be saddled with a long position, he is bullish.

- Writing puts has limited risk as the put writer realizes his maximum loss upon assignment. He would be obligated to purchase the underlying at the exercise price. His maximum loss would be limited to the purchase price paid for the underlying upon receiving an assignment notice less the premium received.

15.   **(D)**

Pam has written a Straddle, which means she is short both a call and a put on the same security, same expiration dates, and same strike prices. A Straddle Writer always has two breakeven points and are calculated in the following manner:

Strike Price of Call Option	+ Total Premium	= Upside Breakeven Point
40	+ 9.75	= 49.75

Strike Price of Put Option	- Total Premium	= Downside Breakeven Point
40	- 9.75	= 30.25

It is important to add that a Straddle Writer expects "neutrality" or "lack of volatility". Stated another way, Straddle Writers are neither bullish nor bearish, but expect the stock to stay in a narrow range. So, if asked, Pam would state the following: "Between now and expiration date, I expect AMZN stock to stay within the range of $49.75 and $30.25. In other words, I don't expect AMZN stock to go above $49.75 or below $30.25."

16.   **(A)**

The Chicago Board Options Exchange (CBOE) trades equity options until 3:00pm central time each day. 3:00pm central time is the same as 4:00pm eastern time, as there is a one-hour time difference. Broad-based index options such as the S&P 500 and the Russell 2000 trade each day until 3:15 central time (4:15pm eastern time).

17.   **(C)**

The investor has created a Bullish Diagonal Spread. The key to determining whether the investor is bullish or bearish is focusing on the option with the larger premium. The option with the larger premium is the short (written) MNO Aug 50 put. Since the investor is short the MNO Aug 50 Put, we can make the determination that the investor is bullish. This is also a Diagonal spread, as it consists of the purchase and sale of both puts (or could also be calls) on the same security with different expiration dates and strike prices.

18.   **(C)**

This strategy is a protective call purchase. Gracie has sold POP stock short, and purchases call options as an insurance policy (hedge) to protect against a rise in POP stock. The breakeven point can be determined as follows:

Short sale price	- Option Premium	= Breakeven Point
55	- 3	= 52

If MNO stock trades $52, Gracie will have made $3/share on the short sale, recouping the premium paid for the call options.

19.   **(C)**

You should be able to identify the position as a short Straddle. The Straddle Writer is short both a call and a put on the same security, same expiration dates, and same strike prices, and expects "neutrality" or "lack of volatility". Stated another way, straddle writers are neither bullish nor bearish, but expect the stock to stay in a narrow range. Now take a closer look at the question:

Ted has two breakeven points: $36.25 and 23.75 (strike price of call + total premium) and the (strike price of the put – total premium). So, at $36.25 and $23.75, Ted does not have a profit or loss.

Ideally, at expiration, Ted would like the stock to close exactly at $30/share. At $30, both options are at-the-money and would expire worthless. The goal when writing or selling options is to collect the premium with the hopes of the option(s) expiring worthless.

20.   **(A)**

This strategy is a protective call purchase. Marissa has sold ROZ stock short, and purchases call options as an insurance policy (hedge) to protect against a rise in ROZ stock. Unlike a typical short seller that is exposed to unlimited risk, Marissa can exercise her 10 ROZ Oct 60 calls, covering her short position in ROZ stock should the stock rise. For example, if ROZ stock were to rise to infinity:

Marissa would exercise her 10 ROZ Oct 60 calls, effectively covering her 1,000 share position at $60. This would result in a 5-point loss on the short sale or $5,000, plus the $3,000 premium paid. Marissa's maximum loss would be $8,000. This can be summarized as follows:

Transaction	Debit or Credit
Sold short 1,000 ROZ at $55	+$55,000 credit
Bought 10 ROZ Oct 60 calls @ 3	-$3,000 debit
Exercise of calls – Right to buy 1,000 ROZ @ 60	-$60,000 debit
-$8,000 loss	

21. **(C)**

William has sold 2 naked call options. As a call writer, William's breakeven point is $82/share. The formula for the breakeven on the sale or purchase of a call is:

Strike Price	+ Premium	= Breakeven Point
80	+ 2	= $82

Just prior to expiration, the call buyer would exercise his options since they would be in-the-money. William would receive an assignment notice which would obligate him to sell 200 shares of XYZ stock at the exercise price of $80. Since William does not own the stock, he would first need to go out to the market and purchase the stock at $82 before selling the stock at the strike price of $80. As a result of exercise and assignment, William would lose 2 points per share which would be offset by his 2 point premium received.

22. **(B)**

The maximum loss for the purchaser of a put (or call) is the premium paid. Josh paid a premium (or debit) of $600, and that is his maximum potential loss. The premium is calculated as follows:

Premium	X Number of Contracts	X Contract Size	= $Premium ($debit)
6	X 1	X 100	= $600

23. **(D)**

Premiums are determined by supply and demand, or market forces. The Options Clearing Corporation ("OCC") issues and guarantees all option contracts. The following features are standardized or fixed by the OCC:

- the security
- strike price
- expiration date

24.　**(B)**

Net debit vertical call spreads and net credit vertical put spreads are both bullish spreads. Let us review each strategy separately:

Bullish Vertical Debit Call Spread	
Bullish Position – overall the investor is bullish as more money or a larger premium is on the bullish side of the market	Buy 1 DEF June 50 Call = 5
Bearish Position	Sell 1 DEF June 55 Call = 3
	Net Debit = 2

Bullish Vertical Credit Put Spread	
Bearish	Buy 1 DEF June 50 Put = 3
Bullish Position – overall the investor is bullish as more money or a larger premium is on the bullish side of the market	Sell 1 DEF June 55 Put = 5
	Net Credit = 2

25.　**(D)**

Mr. Walck has written a naked or uncovered call. Theoretically, the underlying stock could rise to infinity. The call option would be exercised by the buyer, which means that the naked call writer would receive an assignment notice which would trigger the obligation to sell the stock at the strike price. Since the naked call writer does not own the underlying stock, he would first need to purchase the stock in the market at an infinite price and then sell the stock at the strike price. Naked or uncovered call writing is only suitable for investors that understand and are willing to assume unlimited risk.

26.　**(D)**

The AMZN Sept 140 put would be in-the-money or have intrinsic value if the AMZN stock traded $138.25. Put options are in-the-money or have intrinsic value when exercise price is above the market price of the underlying stock.

Choices A and B are scenarios when the AMZN Sept 140 put would be out-of-the money or have zero intrinsic value. Choice C is a scenario in which the AMZN Sept 140 put would be at-the-money.

27.　**(D)**

Gary would break even when the Swiss Franc trades 97.45. The formula for calculating the breakeven point of a put is:

Strike Price	- Premium	= Breakeven Point
100	- 2.55	= 97.45

28.　**(A)**

A long call or the purchase of a call option has unlimited gain potential. Theoretically, the underlying security could rise to infinity and the call buyer could exercise the call, purchasing the underlying stock at the exercise price, and selling the stock in the market at an infinite price.

29.   **(B)**

The key word in the question is "narrow range". The straddle writer is short both a call(s) and a put(s) on the same security, expiration dates, strike prices; the straddle writer expects "neutrality" or "lack of volatility". Stated another way, straddle writers are neither bullish nor bearish, but expect the stock to stay in a narrow range. Let us review an example:

A customer writes 1 XOM Dec 80 straddle at 7. The customer has two breakeven points which can be expressed as follows:

Strike Price of Call Option	+ Total Premium	= Upside Breakeven Point
80	+ 7	= 87

Strike Price of Put Option	- Total Premium	= Downside Breakeven Point
80	-7	= 73

So, the customer has two breakeven points: $87/share and $73/share, and expects XOM to trade within this range. Ideally, at expiration, the customer would like the stock to be exactly at $80/share. At $80, both options would be at-the-money (zero intrinsic value) and would expire worthless.

30.   **(A)**

The investor has created a Bullish Vertical Debit Call Spread. Let's take a closer look at the position.

Bullish Vertical Debit Call Spread	
Bullish Position – even though premiums are not used in this question, the call option with the lower strike price (given the same expiration date) would command a higher premium in the market; the investor is bullish since more money or a larger premium is on the bullish side of the market.	Buy 1 MSFT DEC 25 Call
Bearish Position	Sell 1 MSFT DEC 30 Call
	Net Debit (the premium for the purchase would be larger than the premium for the sale, resulting in a net debit or net purchase)

31.   **(B)**

Patricia's two transactions are as follows:

Transactions		Premium	X Contract Size	X Number of Contracts	= $Premium
Opening Sale	Wrote 3 AMZN July 150 Puts	5	100	3	+ $1,500 (credit)
Closing Purchase	Bought 3 AMZN July 150 Puts	5.50	100	3	-$1,650 (debit)
					-$150 loss

The result of the two transactions is a loss of $150. Note that "liquidate" in this scenario means to close out the transaction with a sale.

32.   **(B)**

The formula for determining the breakeven point for a put is as follows:

Strike Price	- Premium	= Breakpoint
75	- 3	= 72

Mr. Duffy's breakpoint is $72/share. If MNO trades $72/share, Mr. Duffy could:

1) buy 300 shares of MNO stock at the market price of $72;
2) exercise his 3 put options which gives him the right to sell his 300 shares of MNO at the strike price of $75.

These two transactions would result in a profit of 3 points, recouping his 3 point premium. In other words, at $72, the put options would have 3 points of intrinsic value, recouping his 3-point premium.

33.   **(B)**

Ryan received an assignment notice which obligates him to buy the Japanese Yen at the strike price of 120. We can determine Ryan's aggregate cost as follows:

Exercise Price (move decimal FOUR places to the left on the Yen)	X Contract Size	X Number of Contracts	= $ Aggregate Cost
.0120	X 1,000,000	X 1	$12,000

Note, we first must move the decimal point on the exercise price FOUR places to the left. Additionally, the contract size of the Yen is 1,000,000. On all other foreign currencies tested on the Series 7 exam, the decimal point on the exercise price is moved TWO places to the left, and the contract sizes are 10,000.

34.   **(B)**

Short stock and a short put is a covered put writing strategy. Covered put writing entails unlimited risk as the stock could theoretically rise to infinity. The unlimited risk arises from the short stock position. The short put would only provide protection limited to the premium received.

The term "covered" in this context is misleading and does not mean 'safe'. "Covered" in this context means covered for margin purposes as the margin requirement would be limited to 50% of the short sale. No margin requirement is imposed on the sale of the put option.

35.   **(C)**

Initially, the client's cost basis is equal to his premium paid. Note, two contacts were purchased which equals a premium of $600. If later the client exercises his calls, his cost basis will be adjusted to include the aggregate exercise price plus the premium paid.

36.   **(C)**

The Regulation T Payment Date is trade date + five business days or T + 5. If instead, the question asked for the settlement, the answer would be T + 1. We can summarize this as follows:

Regulation T Payment Date	T + 5
Settlement Date	T + 1

37.   **(D)**

While the question asks you to determine the time value, we must first determine if the options have any intrinsic value first.

Seymour's call options have two points of intrinsic value. Call options have intrinsic value or money value when the market price of the underlying stock is above the exercise price or strike price. That difference is the intrinsic value or money value of two points. The remaining portion of the premium equal to 5 points can be attributed to time value, which can be expressed as follows:

Premium	-	Intrinsic Value	= Time Value
7	-	2	= 5

38.   **(B)**

A long call option can be used to protect a short stock position. This strategy is called a Protective Call Purchase. Here is an example:

Short stock position	Short 100 ABC at $50/share
Long call option	Buy 1 ABC July 55 call = 3

The above position has limited risk. If ABC stock rises above $55, the investor can exercise his call, covering his short stock position. His maximum loss would be limited to $800 which can be determined as follows:

Short stock position	Short 100 ABC at $50/share	+ $5,000 credit
Long call option	Buy 1 ABC July 55 call = 3	-$300 debit
Exercise of call	Buy 100 ABC at $55/share	-$5,500
Result = -$800 loss		

39.   **(C)**

The strike price of a yield-based option is actually a yield as opposed to a price. For example, a yield-based put option with a strike price of 4 is actually a yield of 4% (4/100 = 4%). The investor is speculating that the yield of the underlying bond will fall below 4. If instead, the investor purchased a yield-based call option with a strike price of 4, he is speculating that the yield of the underlying security will rise above 4%.

So, if interest rates decline, premiums of yield-based put options will increase and yield-based call options will decline.

40.   **(B)**

The CBOE Gold Index is an example of a narrow-based index option since it is a benchmark for a single commodity. Narrow-based indices can also be based on a single sector of the market. Narrow-based index options cease trading at 4:00pm eastern time, while broad-based index options cease trading at 4:15pm eastern time. We can summarize as follows:

Type of Option	Trading day ends at...
Narrow-based Index Options	4:00pm eastern time
Broad-based Index Options	4:15pm eastern time

41.   **(A)**

The premium equates to a purchase price of $3,437.50. To determine the premium, you will need to know the following:

- T-Bond (T-Note) options are quoted as a percentage of par value + 32nds
- Par value or the contract size is $100,000
- The value of 1/32 is equal to $31.25 ($1,000/32 = $31.25)

We can determine the premium as follows:

Premium		X number of contracts	= $Total Premium
3.14			
(3% x par value)	+ 14/32		
(3% x $100,000)	+ 14 X $31.25		
$3,000	+ $437.50		
$3,437.50		X 1	= $3,437.50

42. **(B)**

Scott's maximum loss when purchasing two puts is limited to the premium paid. Since Scott paid $600 for the two put options, his maximum loss is limited to $200. It can be determined as follows:

Premium	X Number of Contracts	X Contract Size	= $Premium
3	X 2	100	= $600

43. **(A)**

A short stock position or selling short has unlimited risk potential. Theoretically, the stock could rise to infinity where the short seller would cover or buy back the stock, covering his short position.

Writing uncovered or naked call options would also have unlimited risk. The writer of a naked call option has the obligation to sell the underlying stock at the strike price or exercise price if exercised by the buyer. Since the writer of a naked call does not own the underlying stock, if exercised by the holder, he would have to first to out to the market and purchase the stock in order to take the next step and sell to the holder or buyer.

Writing covered calls has limited risk. Unlike the naked call writer described above, the covered call writer owns (hence covered) the underlying stock. If the call is exercised by the buyer (holder), the covered call writer will sell the stock that he already owns at the strike price (exercise price)

44. **(D)**

The investor has created a Covered Put Writing strategy. The Regulation T margin requirement is limited to 50% of the short sale or $20,000. There is no additional margin requirement on the sale of the put options. Note, if the question instead asked for the "cash deposit", the answer would be $35,000 (50% margin requirement on the short sale minus the premium of $5,000 received for writing the put options).

45. **(D)**

The investor's cost basis is the aggregate exercise price + the premium paid. The investor exercised the call option for $5,000, and paid a $300 premium for the call. The investor's cost basis on IBM stock is $5,300.

46. **(D)**

The investor initiates or opens a position by writing calls. This is an example of an opening sale. The position is also uncovered or naked since the investor does not own JTU stock. On the Series 7 exam, if the question does not include any additional information on the investor holding the underlying security, you can assume the investor does not own the underlying security.

47. **(B)**

The holder of a put option has the right to sell the underlying stock, not buy the underlying stock upon exercise. Calls, Rights, and Warrants all give the holder to buy the underlying stock upon exercise.

48. **(C)**

The Options Clearing Corporation ("OCC") utilizes a random selection method when allocating an assignment notice to a broker-dealer. On the other hand, a broker-dealer may utilize a random selection method or a First-In, First-Out Basis (oldest position) when allocating an assignment notice to one of its customers.

49.   **(B)**

The formula for determining the breakeven point for a call option is as follows:

Strike Price	+ Premium	= Breakpoint
75	+3	= 78

Atwood breaks even when XON stock trades $78/share. At $78, the buyer of the call would exercise his right to buy XON stock at $75. As a writer, Atwood would be obligated to sell 300 shares at $75. Since he does not own XON stock he would first go out to the market and purchase it at $78, resulting in a 3 point loss. This 3 point loss would be offset by the 3 point premium received for writing the options, resulting in no gain nor loss to Atwood.

50.   **(C)**

Writing or selling a naked call option entails unlimited risk, regardless of whether the underlying is a currency, yield, bond, equity, or index. All other positions entail limited risk.

OPTIONS EXAM 4

1. Which of the following strategies is most appropriate for a conservative investor with the objective of income generation?

   (A) Long stock + short call
   (B) Long stock + short put
   (C) Long call + long put
   (D) Short stock + short put

2. Max just wrote an XYZ Oct 75 put at 3. In which of the following scenarios would Max achieve the maximum gain? At expiration, XYZ stock is trading:

   I.   Below its strike price
   II. Above its strike price
   III. At its strike price

   (A) I only
   (B) II only
   (C) I and III only
   (D) II and III only

3. An investor is long an ABC July 75 call. The addition of which of the following positions would create a long combination? Long an:

   (A) ABC July 70 put
   (B) ABC July 75 put
   (C) ABD July 70 put
   (D) ABD July 75 put

4. All of the following strategies can be executed in a cash account EXCEPT:

   (A) sale of a put with a deposit of cash equivalent to the aggregate strike price
   (B) sale of a call with a deposit of cash equivalent to the aggregate strike price
   (C) purchase of a call and a put on the same security, strike prices, and expiration dates
   (D) purchase of a call and a put on the same security, different strike prices, and the same expiration dates

5. The OCC issues the AMZN July 160 puts. Once these options begin trading, what are possibilities for the holder of the option contract?

   I.   Exercise
   II. Conversion
   III. Expiration

   (A) I and II only
   (B) I and III only
   (C) II and III only
   (D) III and IV only

6. Marc buys 10 GEC Sept 65 calls at 4. One week later, the calls are sold at 4.35. What is Marc's resulting profit?

   (A) $3,500 profit
   (B) $4,350 profit
   (C) $350 profit
   (D) $35 profit

7. Under which of the following circumstances are options' strike prices not adjusted?

   (A) Odd stock splits
   (B) Even stock splits
   (C) Cash dividends
   (D) Stock dividends

8. Which of the following options would best protect a long stock position?

   (A) Long call
   (B) Short call
   (C) Long put
   (D) Short put

9. Bill buys an XYZ Apr 30 put at 2. Which two of the following characteristics accurately describe Bill's position?

    I.   Bullish
    II. Bearish
    III. Unlimited gain potential
    IV. Limited gain potential

    (A) I and III
    (B) I and IV
    (C) II and III
    (D) II and IV

10. A RR just recommended that his customer write Straddles on a NYSE-listed stock. In which of the following situations would this recommendation be unsuitable for his customer?

    (A) The RR was unable to determine that the customer understood the risks associated with the strategy
    (B) The ROP did not approve the recommendation
    (C) The Firm's research team has not included the stock on its recommended list
    (D) The customer does not have a minimum of ten years of options trading experience

11. Which of the following strategies has the greatest degree of risk?

    (A) Bearish put spread
    (B) Bearish call spread
    (C) Writing combinations
    (D) Writing naked puts

12. A customer initiates an option position by going long 5 ABC Oct 60 calls. How should the RR mark the order ticket?

    (A) Opening sale
    (B) Opening purchase
    (C) Closing sale
    (D) Closing purchase

13. Keith is contemplating the purchase of call options on BCP stock. Which one of the following options would have the smallest premium?

    (A) June 80 calls
    (B) June 85 calls
    (C) June 70 calls
    (D) June 75 calls

14. Broker-Dealer X is assigned an exercise notice by the OCC. Broker-Dealer X has 40 customers which have a short position in this particular option series. In selecting a customer to that will receive an assignment notice, Broker-Dealer X may use any of the following methods EXCEPT:

    (A) random selection
    (B) any method deemed fair and equitable
    (C) smallest position
    (D) oldest position

15. All of the following are examples of broad-based index options EXCEPT:

    (A) S&P 100 Index Options
    (B) CBOE Oil Index Options
    (C) Russell 2000 Index Options
    (D) Nasdaq 100 Index Options

16. A customer's account was just approved for options trading. How many days does the customer have to return an executed options agreement to the firm?

    (A) 15 days
    (B) 10 days
    (C) 5 days
    (D) 20 days

17. Mary goes long 1 XYZ May 40 put at 3 and 1 XYZ May 45 call at 4.5. What is Mary's maximum gain?

    (A) $750
    (B) Unlimited
    (C) $450
    (D) $300

18. An investor goes long an ABC May 70 Straddle for a total premium of 6. All of the following are true EXCEPT:

    (A) the investor will breakeven at $76
    (B) the investor had an initial debit of $600.
    (C) the investor would like ABC stock to close at $70 by expiration
    (D) the investor will earn a profit at $63

19. Kurt goes long 3 ZYZ June 45 put at 3 and also buys 1 ZYZ June 45 call at 3. At what price does the underlying stock need to trade for Kurt to generate a profit?

    (A) $51
    (B) $39
    (C) $50.75
    (D) $38.75

20. Hale, Patty, and Murphy would like to open an options account with your firm. All three parties have extensive experience trading options. Pursuant to SRO rules, account information would need to be collected on:

    (A) all of the parties
    (B) none of the three parties
    (C) two of the three parties
    (D) one of the three parties

21. An investor placed the following trades in his margin account:

    Sell 1 TUV May 60 put at 5
    Buy 100 PQR stock at $40
    Sell 1 PQR Apr 40 call at 3.
    Sell short 100 TUV stock at $60

    What is investor's cash deposit?

    (A) $5,800
    (B) $5,000
    (C) $4,200
    (D) $10,800

22. Markus writes a KLO Feb 25 call at 3 and also writes 1 KLO Feb 25 put at 2. What are Markus's break even points?

    I. $30
    II. $28
    III. $20
    IV. $23

    (A) I and III
    (B) I and IV
    (C) II and III
    (D) II and IV

23. Debra goes long 2 SOX Nov 80 calls at a premium of 2. At what price does the underlying stock need to trade for Debra to break even?

    (A) $84
    (B) $82
    (C) $76
    (D) $78

24. Scott goes short 3 ABC Oct 65 calls and also goes short 3 ABC Oct 65 puts. What is Scott's outlook for ABC stock? He:

    (A) expects neutrality
    (B) is bearish
    (C) is bullish
    (D) expects volatility

25. Dave buys 100 shares of ABX at $26. He also buys 1 ABX June 25 put at 3. At what price does Dave break even?

    (A) $23
    (B) $29
    (C) $28
    (D) $22

26. An investor that decides to purchase OEX (S&P 100) index call options to speculate would not be subject to which two of the following risks?

   I. Market risk
   II. Company risk
   III. Industry risk
   IV Liquidity risk

   (A) I only
   (B) III only
   (C) II and III only
   (D) III and IV only

27. A customer buys a QRS Mar 60 call and sells a QRS June 65 call. What is the name of this strategy?

   (A) Horizontal spread
   (B) Combination spread
   (C) Vertical spread
   (D) Diagonal spread

28. Pam is short 1 AMZN Apr 40 put at 5 and also short 1 AMZN Apr 40 call at 4.75. What is her maximum loss?

   (A) $650
   (B) $975
   (C) $1,950
   (D) Unlimited

29. Dave is the holder of 5 XYZ Mar 40 puts. Shortly after the purchase, XYZ stock splits 4 for 1. Following the split, which of the following correctly reflects Dave's position?

   (A) 5 XYZ Mar 10 puts; 400 shares per contract
   (B) 20 XYZ Mar 10 puts; 100 shares per contract
   (C) 1.25 XYZ Mar 40 puts; 100 shares per contract
   (D) 1.25 XYZ Mar 10 puts; 400 shares per contract

30. Which one of the following is a correct statement regarding adjustment of an options contract for an even stock split? The exercise price is:

   (A) increased
   (B) decreased.
   (C) cancelled
   (D) unchanged

31. An investor is short 2 DEF July 15 calls. He can liquidate his position by entering which one of the following transactions?

   (A) Buy 2 DEF July 15 calls
   (B) Buy 3 DEF July 15 calls
   (C) Buy 2 DEF June 15 calls
   (D) Buy 2 DEF June 10 calls

32. The Russell 2000 Index (RUT) is currently trading at 805. Which one of the following RUT options is out-of-the-money?

   (A) Aug 810 puts
   (B) Aug 800 puts
   (C) Nov 795 calls
   (D) Nov 800 calls

33. Victor goes long 5 XON Oct 75 calls at a premium of 3. He later exercises the call options when the underlying stock is trading at $77 and immediately liquidates the stock in the market. What is Victor's resulting profit or loss?

   (A) $300 loss
   (B) $200 gain
   (C) $500 loss
   (D) $500 gain

34. A customer buys a POP Apr 60 put at 7 and writes a POP Apr 55 put at 4. The customer would earn a profit in all of the following scenarios EXCEPT:

   (A) the spread narrows
   (B) POP common stock declines sharply
   (C) the spread widens
   (D) both puts are deep in-the-money at expiration

35. Which of the following factor(s) contribute to the time value of an option?

   I.   Intrinsic value of the option
   II. Length of time until expiration
   III. Volatility of the underlying stock

   (A) I only
   (B) II only
   (C) I and II only
   (D) II and III only

36. Which strategy entails the greatest risk of the four?

   (A) Short put
   (B) Short straddle
   (C) Long call
   (D) Covered call writing

37. Mr. Murray buys 10 JKL Nov 20 calls at 3. What is Mr. Murray's maximum potential loss?

   (A) Unlimited
   (B) $2,300
   (C) $3,000
   (D) $300

38. Five months ago, a customer of Capital Advisors LLC sold short 500 shares of PFE stock at $40. The stock is currently trading at $28, and he decides to purchase 5 PFE Oct 45 calls for 3. What are the consequences of purchasing these call options?

   (A) He has created a hedge
   (B) His position is now bullish
   (C) If the stock trades above $45 by the end of October, his calls expire worthless.
   (D) This is an income-generating strategy

39. Marc writes 1 GHI Sept 25 put at 3. What is Marc's break even point?

   (A) $28
   (B) $22
   (C) $25
   (D) $21

40. Which two of the following are the correct contract sizes for foreign currency options?

   I.   Japanese Yen has a contract size of 1,000
   II. British Pound has a contract size of 1,000
   III. Swiss Franc has a contract size of 10,000
   IV. Euro has a contract size of 10,000

   (A) I and II
   (B) I and III
   (C) II and III
   (D) III and IV

41. Which two of the following are true concerning LEAPS?

   I.   Maximum expiration of 39 months
   II. Maximum expiration of 9 months
   III. LEAPS have January expiration dates only
   IV. LEAPS have December expiration dates only

   (A) I and III
   (B) I and IV
   (C) II and III
   (D) II and IV

42. In his cash account, Paul holds 10 MSFT Apr 25 calls in which he deposited $5,000. Five months later, he exercises the calls and immediately sells the stock at $28/share. What will Paul be required to deposit in his account?

   (A) $28,000
   (B) $20,000
   (C) $25,000
   (D) $0

43. A customer buys an RUT (Russell 2000 Index) Oct 805 call for 3. Five months later, the customer exercises the call when the index settles at 807. What is the customer's resulting profit or loss?

   (A) $100 profit
   (B) $100 loss
   (C) $300 loss
   (D) $200 profit

44. An investor sells 1 ABC July 35 call at 3. Which of the following statements best describe the investor's outlook? The investor is:

    (A) bearish and has unlimited potential maximum gain
    (B) bearish and has a potential maximum gain of $300
    (C) bullish and has an unlimited potential maximum gain
    (D) bullish and has a potential maximum gain of $300

45. An options transaction is settled between which of the following counterparties?

    (A) The broker and the contra broker
    (B) The OCC and the clearing broker
    (C) The OCC and the exchange where the option is executed
    (D) The introducing broker and the clearing broker

46. Victor goes long 5 XON Oct 75 calls at a premium of 7. With the stock trading at $77 per share, how much time value do the call options have?

    (A) 5 points
    (B) 7 points
    (C) 2 points
    (D) 0 points

47. Which of the following four strategies is considered moderately bullish?

    (A) Covered call writing
    (B) Naked call writing
    (C) Long combination
    (D) Protective call purchase

48. A customer establishes the following position:

    Long 1 XOM Aug 75 call at 5
    Short 1 XOM Aug 80 call at 3
    Long 100 shares of XOM stock at $75

    What is the customer's maximum loss?

    (A) $7,200
    (B) Unlimited
    (C) $7,700
    (D) $7,500

49. Mr. Jackson establishes the following position in his options account:

    Short 100 shares of DEF at $50
    Short 1 DEF Feb 45 put at 2

    What is Mr. Jackson's maximum loss?

    (A) Unlimited
    (B) $700
    (C) $300
    (D) $500

50. An investor sells short 100 shares of ABC at $25 and also writes 1 ABC Aug 20 put at 3. By the third week of August, ABC stock trades $18 and the investor receives an assignment notice. What is his resulting profit?

    (A) $1,000
    (B) $400
    (C) $200
    (D) $800

OPTIONS EXPLANATIONS 4

1.   (A)

A position consisting of a long stock position + a short call is a covered call writing strategy, which is suitable for an investor with a conservative risk profile.   The maximum loss is limited to the amount paid for the stock minus the premium received for writing the option.

This is also an income-generating strategy as the call is written to generate additional income. This strategy is common with dividend paying stocks. The investor receives dividend income from the underlying stock in addition to the premium income received for writing the option.

2.   (D)

As a Put Writer, Max would achieve the maximum gain if the put option expires worthless. If XYZ stock is trading above the strike price (out-of-the-money) or at the strike price (at-the-money), the put option would expire worthless. Ideally, the writer of any option would like to collect the premium income from selling the option with the hope of the option expiring worthless.

3.   (A)

The addition of a long ABC July 70 put would create a long Combination, which consists of the purchase or sale of both a call and a put on the same security with different expiration dates and/or strike prices. The Combination buyer (like a Straddle buyer) expects volatility.

Choice B is incorrect as the additional position would create a Straddle. Choices C and D are incorrect as the security is "ABD" and not "ABC" as in the question.

4.   (B)

This is an Except question. The sale of a call with a deposit of cash equivalent to the aggregate strike price is still a naked or uncovered call writing strategy, which entails unlimited risk and can only be executed in a margin account. In other words, the investor's risk is not limited to a deposit of cash equal to the aggregate strike price.

Choice A is a covered put writing strategy. Under the worst possible scenario, the investor would be obligated to purchase the stock at the strike price. The investor has cash equivalent to the aggregate strike price to cover his position.

Choice C is the purchase of a Straddle, while Choice D is the purchase of a Combination. With both of these strategies, the most the investor could lose is the total debit for the purchase of the call and put.

5.   **(B)**

The holder or buyer of an option will experience one of three possible outcomes during the life of the option:

- Exercise - The holder of an option has the ability to exercise the option. In the case of a call option, the holder has a right to buy the underlying instrument (stock, currency, etc).
- Liquidation - The holder may liquidate or close out his or her option contract on the secondary market (CBOE, PHILX, AMEX) any time prior to expiration.
- Expiration - all options have an expiration date. If the holder does not exercise or liquidate his or her option, it will expire on the Saturday following the third Friday at 11:59pm of the expiration month.

Roman numeral choice II, "conversion", is not a possibility as the put option cannot be converted to AMZN stock.

6.   **(C)**

Mark earns a $350 profit. The profit is calculated as follows:

Transaction	Premium	X Number of Contracts	X Contract Size	= $Premium
Bought 10 GEC Sept 65 calls	4	X 10	X 100	= -$4,000 (debit)
Sold 10 GEC Sept 65 calls	4.35	X 10	X 100	= $4,350 (credit)
Result = $350 profit				

7.   **(C)**

Strike prices or exercise prices are not adjusted for cash dividends. It is important to note that adjustments to the strike price of an option contract are made for stock dividends and stock splits (both even and odd).

8.   **(C)**

A Long put would be the best method of protecting or hedging a long position. A Protective Put Purchase consists of a long stock position and a long put(s). A Long put is used only as an insurance policy to protect against a decline in the long position. Under the worst possible outcome, the investor's put option allows for the sale of his stock at the exercise price or strike price.

9.   **(D)**

The purchase of a put has limited gain potential. Bill is bearish as the purchaser of a put and can only profit from the strike price (30) to zero, less the premium paid. If XYZ stock fell to zero, Bill could purchase the stock at zero and exercise his put, which would allow him to sell his stock at $30/share. He would then make a profit of 30 points less the 2 point premium.

10.   **(A)**

A registered representative (RR) that makes a recommendation to a customer without fully understanding the risks associated with the strategy is automatically in violation of the suitability rule. An RR cannot make a suitability determination if she does not understand the strategy herself. This is true even if the recommendation is appropriate for the customer.

11.   **(C)**

The Combination Writer is short both a call and a put on the same security, different expiration dates and/or strike prices. The key point is that embedded in the Combination Writers position is a naked call option, which lends the position to unlimited risk. Theoretically, the underlying stock could rise to infinity. The call option would be exercised by the buyer. This means the Combination Writer would receive an assignment notice which would trigger the obligation to sell the stock at the strike price. Since he does not own the underlying stock, it would first need to be purchased in the market at an infinite price and then sold at the strike price.

12.   **(B)**

The question states that the customer "initiates", which means he or she has engaged in an "opening" transaction and initiates the position by going 'long", which is a "purchase". To liquate his long position of 5 ABC Oct 60 calls, the customer would need to engage in a closing sale.

13.   **(B)**

Since the expiration dates are all the same, the call option with the highest strike price would have the smallest premium. In the hands of the buyer, the call option which gives the buyer the right to buy 100 shares of BCP stock 85 would be the least valuable while the June 70 calls would be the most valuable. This is also true from the writer's perspective, as the June 70 call would command the largest premium and the June 85 call would command the smallest premium.

14.   **(C)**

Assignment based upon the smallest position (and largest position) is considered to be discriminatory. All other choices are considered to fair methods for allocating assignment notices.

15.   **(B)**

The CBOE Oil Index Option is considered to be narrow based, as it is limited to one commodity or sector of the market. Broad-based indices such as the S&P 100, Russell 2000, and Nasdaq 100 are diversified across various industries.

16.   **(A)**

After a customer's account has been approved by a Registered Options Principal (ROP), the customer has 15 days to return an executed options agreement to the firm. If an executed agreement is not received by the firm within 15 days, the customer is only permitted to engage in closing transactions, or otherwise liquidate an existing position.

17.   **(B)**

Mary has created a long combination, which consists of the purchase of a put and call on the same security, with different expiration dates and/or strike price. Mary's maximum gain is unlimited since the position involves the purchase of a call option.

18.   **(C)**

The investor has created a Long Straddle. The straddle buyer is long both a call and a put on the same security, expiration dates, strike prices, and expects "volatility" in the underlying security. Stated another way, straddle buyers are neither bullish nor bearish, but expect the stock to fluctuate in a wide range.

Let's take a closer look at this example. The investor buys 1 ABC May 70 Straddle at 6. The breakeven points of $76/share and $64/share can be determined as follows:

Strike Price of Call Option	+ Total Premium	= Upside Breakeven Point
70	+ 6	= 76

Strike Price of Put Option	- Total Premium	= Downside Breakeven Point
70	- 6	= 64

So, Choice A is correct as one of the two breakeven points is $76/share. Choice D is also correct as the investor will earn a profit if ABC stock trades below his downside breakeven point of $64. Choice B is also correct as the investor has an initial debit of $600 or 6 points.

Since this is an "Except" question, the only false statement is "C". If the stock closes at $70 at expiration, both the put and the call would expire worthless, yielding the investor the maximum loss of $600, his debit.

19.   **(D)**

You should be able to identify the position as a Long Straddle. The straddle buyer is long both a call and a put on the same security, expiration dates, and strike prices. The straddle buyer expects "volatility" in the underlying security.

Kurt buys 3 ZYZ June 45 straddles at 6.   While the question asks you to solve for a "profit", we must first determine the breakeven points which can be determined as follows:

Strike Price of Call Option	+ Total Premium	= Upside Breakeven Point
45	+ 6	= 51

Strike Price of Put Option	- Total Premium	= Downside Breakeven Point
45	- 6	= 39

As a Straddle buyer, Kurt expects volatility, which means he will earn a profit above $51/share or below $39/share. Choice "D" is correct as Kurt generates a profit $38.75 since the stock would be trading below its breakeven of $39.

20.   **(A)**

Under the "Know Your Customer" rule of the CBOE, information must be collected on all parties on the account. When determining if a trade is suitable for the account, the transaction must be appropriate for all parties.

21. **(C)**

The four positions can be rearranged into two strategies. The key in determining that these are two strategies is to match the two positions that have the same security:

- PQR – Covered Call Writing
- TUV – Covered Put Writing

Covered Call Writing Strategy	
Buy 100 PQR stock at $40	Margin requirement 50% = $2,000
Sell 1 PQR Apr 40 call at 3	Premium received = $300
Cash deposit is equal to the margin requirement on the stock position – premium received	Cash deposit = $1,700

Covered Put Writing Strategy	
Sell short 100 TUV stock at $60	Margin requirement 50% = $3,000
Sell 1 TUV May 60 put at 5	Premium received = $500
Cash deposit is equal to the margin requirement on the stock position – premium received	Cash deposit = $2,500

We can then add the cash deposit for the covered call writing strategy ($1,700) and the covered put writing strategy ($2,500) for a total cash deposit of $4,200.

22. **(A)**

Markus has written a straddle, which means he is short both a call and a put on the same security, expiration dates, and strike prices. A straddle writer always has two breakeven points, calculated in the following manner:

Strike Price of Call Option	+ Total Premium	= Upside Breakeven Point
25	+ 5	= 30

Strike Price of Put Option	- Total Premium	= Downside Breakeven Point
25	- 5	= 20

So, Markus breaks even at $30/share and $20/share.

It is important to add that a straddle writer expects "neutrality" or "lack of volatility". Stated another way, straddle writers are neither bullish nor bearish, but expect the stock to stay in a narrow range. So if asked, Markus would state the following: "Between now and the expiration date of the options, I expect KO stock to stay within the range of $30/share and $20/share. In other words, I don't expect KO stock to go above $30 or below $20/share."

23. **(B)**

The breakeven point on a call option is the strike price + premium. Debra would break even when the underlying stock trades $82. At $82, Debra could exercise her call options, and purchase SOX stock at $80. Following the exercise, she could then sell her stock in the market at $82. Her 2-point profit would be offset against her 2-point premium for the options, resulting in no gain or loss.

24. **(A)**

Scott has written a straddle, which means he is short both a call and a put on the same security, same expiration dates, and same strike prices. A straddle writer expects "neutrality" or "lack of volatility". Stated another way, straddle writers are neither bullish nor bearish, but expect the stock to stay in a narrow range. A straddle writer has two breakeven points, which means that Scott does not expect ABC stock to go above or below the breakeven points.

25. **(B)**

The position is a Protective Put Purchase, which consists of a long stock position and a long put(s). Dave is long 1 ABX puts only as an insurance policy to protect against a decline in his long ABX stock position. His breakeven point can be determined as follows:

Purchase price of stock	+ Premium of put	= Breakeven Point
$26	+ 3	= $29

So, Dave needs ABX stock to rise to $29/share to recoup the 3-point premium paid for the puts. So, at $29/share, the following would result: Dave's ABX stock which was purchased at $26 is sold at $29, resulting in a 3-point profit. The 3-point profit on the sale of the stock is offset against the 3-point premium paid for the put options. The result is no gain or loss.

26. **(C)**

An investor that purchases the OEX would not be subject to company risk, also known as company specific risk, as the index is diversified across one hundred different companies. An investor would also not be subject to industry risk, as the index is diversified across many different sectors or industries. Therefore, there is no one company or industry that should have a detrimental affect on the OEX.

27. **(D)**

The name of this strategy is a Diagonal spread, meaning that it consists of the purchase or sale of both calls or puts on the same security with different expiration dates and/or strike prices.

28. **(D)**

Pam is a straddle writer, which means she is short both a call and a put on the same security, same expiration dates, and same strike prices. The key point is that embedded in the straddle writers position is a naked or uncovered call option that lends the position to unlimited risk. Theoretically, the underlying stock could rise to infinity. The call option would be exercised by the buyer. This means the straddle writer (Pam) would receive an assignment notice which would trigger the obligation to sell AMZN stock at the strike price. Since Pam does not own AMZN stock, it would first need to be purchased in the market at an infinite price and then sold at the strike price of $40/share.

Like the naked call writer, the straddle writer has unlimited risk, and is only suitable for investors that understand and are willing to assume such risk.

29.　**(B)**

The first step in the process is being able to identify an even stock split, which always ends with a ratio of 1. Examples include 2 for 1, 3 for 1, 4 for 1, and 5 for 1. In the case of a 4 for 1 stock split, each shareholder will receive four shares for each share that they own.

Option contracts are also affected in that the exercise price decreases while the number of contracts increases proportionally. Dave owns 5 XYZ Mar 40 puts. Following the split, he now owns 20 XYZ Mar 10 puts. Note the number of contracts increases while the exercise price or strike price decreases proportionally. Twenty contracts (4/1 x 5 original contract), 10 exercise price (1/4 x 40 exercise price). It is also important to note the aggregate exercise price remains the same before and after the split at $20,000.

30.　**(B)**

An Even Stock Split always ends with a ratio of 1. Examples include: 2 for 1, 3 for 1, 4 for 1, and 5 for 1. After an Even Split, the exercise price is decreased while the number of option contracts increases. It is also important to note the aggregate exercise price remains the same before and after an Even Split.

31.　**(A)**

The customer would like to "liquidate" or "close out" his existing short position consisting of 2 DEF July 15 calls. To do so, he will need to engage in a "closing purchase". Since he initially "sold" or "wrote" two options, he would now need to purchase two options that are of the same series (same security, expiration date, strike price, and type), and consisting of the same number of contracts.

The other three choices are incorrect since either the number of contracts, expiration date, or strike price have been varied.

It is important to remember that liquidating is synonymous with closing. However, liquidating may require the sale or purchase, depending upon what the initial position consisted of.

32.　**(B)**

A put option is out-of-the-money or has no intrinsic value when the market price of the underlying (e.g. – index, security, currency) is above the strike price. Since the Russell 2000 Index is above the strike price of the Aug 800 puts (Choice B), that contract is out-of-the-money.

The reverse is true of a call option, which is out-of-the-money or has no intrinsic value when the market price of the underlying (e.g. – index, security, currency) is below the strike price.

33.　**(C)**

We can determine Victor's profit or loss by detailing the three transactions that take place:

Transaction	Debit or Credit
Long (buys) 5 XON Oct 75 calls at 3	-$1,500 debit
Exercise of 5 XON Oct 75 calls	-$37,500 debit
Sale of 500 shares of XON stock at $77	+$38,500 credit
	-$500 loss

34.　　**(A)**

This is an Except question, so you are looking for the Wrong answer.

Since the customer purchased the put option with the higher premium, he is has a net debit (net buyer). When an investor establishes a net debit he would like the spread to widen. Meaning he established the spread at a net debit of 3. If he can unwind or liquidate the position at a price that is greater than 3, he will earn a profit. That would be an example of the spread widening.

From a test taking perspective, we can reduce the possible correct choices to: "The spread narrows" or "The spread widens". It is not possible for the customer to want the spread to both widen and narrow.

35.　　**(D)**

An option's premium is composed of two components:

- Intrinsic value (in-the-money amount)
  　　　　PLUS
- Time Value

The time value component of an option can be broken down further into:

- Length of time until expiration
- Volatility of the underlying stock

So, if two options with different underlying securities have the same intrinsic value and length of time until expiration, the option with the underlying security with greater volatility would command a higher premium in the marketplace.

36.　　**(B)**

The straddle writer is short both a call(s) and a put(s) on the same security, expiration dates, strike prices. The key point is that embedded in the straddle writers position is a naked or uncovered call option, which lends the position to unlimited risk. Theoretically, the underlying stock could rise to infinity. The call option would be exercised by the buyer. This means the straddle writer would receive an assignment notice which would trigger the obligation to sell the stock at the strike price. Since the straddle writer does not own the underlying stock, it would first need to be purchased in the market at an infinite price and then sold at the strike price.

Like the naked call writer, the straddle writer has unlimited risk, and is only suitable for investors that understand and are willing to assume such risk. The other three strategies each entail limited risk: short put, long call, and covered call writing.

37.　　**(C)**

The maximum potential loss to the buyer of a call (or put) is limited to the premium or debit paid. Since Mr. Murray paid $3,000 for his 10 JKL Nov 20 calls, $3,000 is his maximum loss.

38. **(A)**

The customer is hedging or protecting his short position by purchasing call options on PFE stock. Let's compare the unhedged position to the hedged position:

Unhedged Position	Hedged Position
Sold short 500 shares of PFE at $40/share	Sold short 500 shares of PFE at $40/share
	Bought 5 PFE Oct 45 calls at 3
Theoretically, PFE could rise to infinity, leaving the short seller with unlimited risk since he would have to cover his short position in the market	The short seller does not have unlimited risk because the short seller does not have to go out to the market to cover his position; he can simply exercise his call options and cover his short position at the strike price of $45/share.

39. **(B)**

The formula for determining the breakeven point for a put option is:

Strike Price	- Premium	= Breakeven Point
25	-3	= 22

Mark's breakeven point is $22/share. To break even, Mark could purchase the stock in the market at $22/share and exercise his put, giving him the right to sell the stock at $25/share. The 3-point profit earned would be offset against the 3-point premium paid.

40. **(D)**

With only one exception, all foreign currencies tested on the Series 7 exam have a contract size of 10,000. The one exception is the Japanese Yen which has a contract size of 1,000,000.

41. **(A)**

LEAPS (**L**ong- term **E**quity **A**ntici**P**ation of **S**ecurities) is a product of the CBOE. LEAPS are long-term call options with a maximum expiration of 39 months and have January expiration dates only. Standard or regular options have a maximum expiration date of 9 months and may have expiration dates of any month.

42. **(C)**

Even though Paul generated a 3-point profit on the exercise and sale, he is still required to deposit 100% of the exercise price or $25,000. The $5,000 premium initially deposited cannot be offset against the aggregate exercise price. If instead, Paul exercised the MSFT options in his margin account, he would only be required to deposit 50% or $12,500.

43. **(B)**

Let us walk through the transactions that took place to determine our resulting loss:

Transaction	Debit or Credit
Bought 1 RUT Oct 85 Call for 3	-$300 debit
Exercise of RUT Oct 805 Call (Index settled at 807)	+$200
Result = -$100 loss	

44.   **(B)**

The seller or writer of a naked or uncovered call is bearish. The maximum gain is limited to the premium received of $300. The premium can be determined as follows:

Premium	X Number of contracts	X Contract Size	= $Premium
3	X 1	X 100	= $300

45.   **(B)**

An options transaction is settled between the Options Clearing Corporation ("OCC") and the clearing broker-dealer. Once an option transaction is booked and paid for, the OCC acts as counterparty for each buyer and seller. Effectively, counterparty risk is removed.

46.   **(A)**

Before attempting to answer how much time value the options have, we must first determine how much intrinsic value the options have. The call options have 2 points of intrinsic value as the strike price is 75 when XON stock is trading at $77/share. Now that we have determined the intrinsic value, we are now ready to determine the time value of the options:

Premium	- Intrinsic value	= time value
7	-2	= 5

Since the total premium is 7 points, we subtract the intrinsic value of 2 points, and the remaining premium of 5 points is the time value.

47.   **(A)**

Covered call writing is considered a moderately bullish strategy. The investor is long stock and writes a call option against the long stock position. Let's illustrate why this is moderately bullish with an example:

Buy 100 JKL at $50	Bullish position as $5,000 is on the bullish side of the market
Write 1 JKL Aug 55 call at 3	Bearish as a writer receives a $300 premium

Overall, the investor is bullish since more money is positioned on the bullish side of the market ($5,000). We can also make the claim that the investor is "moderately" bullish as opposed to being aggressively bullish. Even though the investor is long JKL stock, he does not have unlimited upside potential. The investor will only profit from $50 (the price he purchased the stock) to $55 as the stock would be called away from him above $55/share. If the investor was aggressively bullish he would not position himself to limit his profit to the $55/share level.

48.   **(D)**

To determine what the customer's maximum loss may be, we first must determine if the customer is bullish or bearish. Let's take a closer look at the position:

Position	Outlook
Long 1 XOM Aug 75 call	Bullish, $500 premium
Short 1 XOM Aug 80 call	Bearish, $300 premium
Long 100 shares of XOM stock	Bullish, $7,500 stock purchase

Overall the investor is bullish, as $8,000 is positioned on the bullish side of the market and only $300 is positioned on the bearish side of the market. So, the worst scenario for a bullish investor is XOM stock declining to zero. If that were to happen, he would lose $8,000 on his bullish positions, but profit by $300 on his bearish position. Netting the bullish positions against the bearish position would result in a loss of $7,500.

49.   **(A)**

This strategy is called Covered Put Writing, which is a misleading term, in that "covered" in this context does not imply safety, but rather means that it is "covered" for margin purposes.

Now, let us take a closer look at Mr. Jackson's position:

Short 100 shares of DEF at $50	Bearish position with unlimited risk
Short 1 DEF Feb 45 put at 2	Bullish position with limited gain potential of $200

Theoretically, if DEF stock rose to infinity, as a short seller, Mr. Jackson would lose an unlimited amount of money. The short put would not provide much protection at all as the maximum gain would be limited to the $200 premium received. Overall, Mr. Jackson would be subject to unlimited risk.

50.   **(D)**

Let's take a closer look at the three transactions that have taken place:

Transaction	Result
Sold short 100 ABC at $25	Receives proceeds of +$2500 (credit)
Wrote 1 ABC Aug 20 put at 3	Receives proceeds of +300 (credit)
Assignment notice – obligates the investor to buy 100 ABC at $20/share	Makes purchase in the amount of -$2,000 (debit)
Net result	$800 net credit or profit

OPTIONS EXAM 5

1. All of the following strategies have limited risk EXCEPT:

   (A) credit Call Spread
   (B) debit Put Spread
   (C) short Combination
   (D) protective Call Purchase

2. Tara buys 2 EBAY Sept 30 puts at 4. Six weeks later, the puts are sold at 3.75. What is the resulting profit or loss?

   (A) $25 profit
   (B) $25 loss
   (C) $50 profit
   (D) $50 loss

3. Debbie goes short 5 XON Oct 75 calls at a premium of 5. With the stock trading at $77 per share, how much intrinsic value do Debbie's calls have?

   (A) 7 points
   (B) 3 points
   (C) -2 points
   (D) 2 points

4. An investor goes long 1 ABC June 40 put at 7. What is his breakeven point?

   (A) $33
   (B) $39
   (C) $40
   (D) $47

5. An investor writes 1 XYZ June 70 put. The addition of which of the following would create a Bullish Vertical spread? Buy 1 XYZ:

   (A) Sept 75 put
   (B) June 75 put
   (C) Sept 75 put
   (D) June 65 put

6. Which one of the following is a correct statement regarding adjustment of an options contract for a "stock dividend"? The number of shares per contracts is:

   (A) increased
   (B) cancelled
   (C) unchanged
   (D) decreased.

7. Which two of the following allocation methods are permissible when allocating an assignment notice by a broker-dealer to one of its customers?

   I.   Random selection
   II. Smallest position
   III. Largest position
   IV   Oldest position

   (A) I and II only
   (B) I and IV only
   (C) II and III only
   (D) II and IV only

8. Where do foreign currency options trade?

   (A) Philadelphia Stock Exchange
   (B) Interbank market
   (C) Philadelphia Options Exchange
   (D) Chicago Board Options Exchange

9. Ed goes long 5 XON Oct 75 calls at a premium of 3. At what price does the underlying stock need to trade for Ed to breakeven?

   (A) $90
   (B) $60
   (C) $78
   (D) $72

10. Trader Joe expects the British Pound to strengthen against the U.S. Dollar. Which of the following strategies would be profitable if Trader Joe were to be correct?

    (A) Buy calls on the British Pound
    (B) Buy puts on the U.S. Dollar
    (C) Buy calls on the U.S. Dollar
    (D) Buy puts on the British Pound

11. All of the following currency options have a contract size of 10,000 EXCEPT:

    (A) Canadian Dollar
    (B) Japanese Yen
    (C) British pound
    (D) Australian Dollar

12. All of the following transactions may be executed in a cash account EXCEPT:

    (A) Buy 1 ABC Nov 55 call, and write 1 ABC Nov 50 call
    (B) Buy 1 ABC Nov 55 put, and write 1 ABC Nov 50 put
    (C) Buy 1 ABC Nov 55 call, and buy 1 ABC Nov 55 put
    (D) Buy 1 ABC Nov 55 call and buy 1 ABC Sept 50 put

13. Taleen sells short 200 ABC at $65. To protect her position, she buys 2 ABC 70 calls at 5. What is Taleen's breakeven point per share?

    (A) $70
    (B) $65
    (C) $75
    (D) $60

14. Bob goes long 1,000 shares of XYZ stock at $50. He also goes long 10 XYZ July 40 puts at 2. At what price does Bob breakeven?

    (A) $38
    (B) $52
    (C) $48
    (D) $42

15. A speculator anticipates the Dollar will strengthen against the Swiss Franc. Which two of the following strategies could the speculator use to profit from his expectation?

    I.   Buy puts on the Swiss Franc
    II. Buy calls on the Swiss Franc
    III. Sell calls on the Swiss Franc
    IV   Sell puts on the Swiss Franc

    (A) I and II
    (B) I and III
    (C) II and IV
    (D) III and IV

16. Time value plus intrinsic value is equal to the:

    (A) strike price.
    (B) premium.
    (C) contract size.
    (D) market value.

17. An investor writes 1 ABC May 35 put at 5. What is his breakeven point?

    (A) $30
    (B) $35
    (C) $29
    (D) $40

18. Mr. Halasi bought 10 DEF Aug 80 puts for 3.50 when the market price for DEF was at $81/share. If DEF stock is trading $83/share at expiration, what is Mr. Halasi's resulting loss?

    (A) $3,000
    (B) $300
    (C) $3,500
    (D) $350

19. Scott is bearish on XON stock. He goes short a July 80 call for a premium of 4 and goes long a July 85 call for 2. Why did Scott purchase a call option on XON stock as opposed to only shorting XON stock? Scott was looking to:

    (A) decrease his maximum loss.
    (B) increase his maximum gain.
    (C) decrease his margin requirement.
    (D) increase the probability of getting his order executed.

20. An investor writes 10 XYZ Sept 50 calls at 5. In all of the following circumstances the investor would be considered covered EXCEPT:

    (A) 1,000 shares of XYZ common stock is held in his bank account
    (B) 1,000 shares of XYZ common stock is held in his brokerage account
    (C) XYZ preferred stock which has been tendered for 1,000 XYZ common stock but has not yet been received is held in his brokerage account
    (D) XYZ convertible bonds in his brokerage account with the privilege to convert into 1,000 common stock shares of XYZ stock

21. MSFT put options are an example of a:

    (A) type
    (B) class
    (C) series
    (D) strategy

22. Tom is the holder of 1 ABC July 60 call. Shortly after the purchase, ABC stock splits 5 for 2. Following the split, which of the following correctly reflects Thomas's position?

    (A) 2.5 ABC July 24 calls; 100 shares per contract
    (B) 1 ABC July 24 call; 250 shares per contract
    (C) 1 ABC June 24 call; 250 shares per contract
    (D) 2.5 ABC July 150 call; 100 shares per contract

23. Marissa sells short 100 PNO at $40, and also writes 1 PNO Nov 35 put at 3. What is Marissa's breakeven point per share?

    (A) $32
    (B) $38
    (C) $37
    (D) $43

24. Tina has purchased 2 ABC Aug 40 calls at 6 and sold 2 ABC Aug 50 calls at 2. What is Tina's breakeven point?

    (A) 36
    (B) 44
    (C) 52
    (D) 46

25. In his cash account, Jack goes long 300 shares of IBM at $42.25 and also goes short 3 IBM Aug 45 calls at a premium of 5. What is Jack's cash deposit?

    (A) $12,675
    (B) $11,175
    (C) $14,175
    (D) $1,500

26. A Swiss exporter is expecting payment from its customer in U.S. dollars. Which two of the following will assist the Swiss exporter in hedging its position?

    I.   Buy Swiss Franc calls
    II. Sell Swiss Franc puts
    III. Buy Swiss Franc puts
    IV   Sell Swiss Franc calls

    (A) I and II
    (B) I and III
    (C) II and IV
    (D) III and IV

27. A customer's account is approved for options trading by the firm's ROP. When does an executed customer agreement need to be received by the Firm in order for the customer to continue trading options?

    (A) Within 10 days of account approval by the ROP
    (B) Within 10 days of executing the initial trade
    (C) Within 15 days of executing the initial trade
    (D) Within 15 days of account approval by the ROP

28. Which of the following are responsibilities of the ROP?

    I.   Reviewing option account activity
    II. Reviewing options advertisements
    III. Reviewing option order tickets

    (A) I only
    (B) I and II only
    (C) II and III only
    (D) I, II, and III

29. An investor exercises an IBM Apr 135 call. How many days following the trade date will settlement take place?

    (A) Same business day
    (B) Next business day
    (C) Three business days
    (D) Five business days

30. The hours of trading for foreign currency options are:

    (A) 9:30am to 4:00pm CST
    (B) 24 hours, 7 days per week
    (C) 9:30am to 4:00pm EST
    (D) 9:30am to 4:00pm PST

31. Julie goes short 10 AMZN Aug 180 puts at 3. Three days later, the puts are liquidated at 2.75. What is the resulting profit or loss?

    (A) $250 profit
    (B) $250 loss
    (C) $2,500 profit
    (D) $2,500 loss

32. Which of the following is a Bull Spread?

    (A) Short a Sept 65 call and long a Sept 70 call
    (B) Short a Sept 65 call and long a Sept 65 call
    (C) Short a Mar 70 call and long a Sept 65 call
    (D) Short a Sept 65 call and long a Sept 70 call

33. Ryan sells short 1,000 EWZ at $55 per share. He also buys 10 EWZ Aug 60 calls at 3. What is Ryan's maximum potential gain?

    (A) $8,000
    (B) $55,000
    (C) Unlimited
    (D) $52,000

34. A speculator anticipates the Dollar will weaken against the Euro. Which two of the following strategies could the speculator use to profit from his expectation?

    I.   Buy puts on the Euro
    II. Buy calls on the Euro
    III. Sell calls on the Euro
    IV   Sell puts on the Euro

    (A) I and II
    (B) I and III
    (C) II and III
    (D) II and IV

35. An investor expects the S&P 500 Index to trade over a wide range over the next six months. Which of the following strategies would be consistent with his expectations?

    (A) Write Straddles
    (B) Buy Combinations
    (C) Buy Vertical spreads
    (D) Buy Horizontal spreads

36. According to industry rules, regular-way settlement for foreign currency options takes place within how many business days of the trade date?

    (A) Two days
    (B) Five days
    (C) Three days
    (D) One day

37. On January 5, 2010 a trader is contemplating the purchase of put options on Ford stock. Which one of the following options would have the largest premium?

    (A) Apr 15 puts
    (B) Feb 20 puts
    (C) Aug 20 puts
    (D) June 15 puts

38. Which of the following option strategies does Not have limited loss potential?

    (A) Short call
    (B) Long put
    (C) Long call
    (D) Short put

39. Exxon Mobil Corporation just declared its quarterly dividend of 33 cents per share. In which two of the following scenarios would the investor receive the dividend?

    I.   A call buyer that exercises his option the day before the ex-dividend date
    II.   A call writer that is assigned an exercise notice the day before the ex- dividend date
    III. A put buyer that exercises his option the day before the ex-dividend date
    IV   A put writer that receives an assignment notice the day before the ex-dividend date

    (A) I and III
    (B) I and IV
    (C) II and III
    (D) II and IV

40. An investor purchases 2 ABC May 65 puts at 3. What is the Regulation T requirement?

    (A) 0%
    (B) 25%
    (C) 100%
    (D) 50%

41. Mr. Simpson establishes the following position in his options account:

    Long 100 shares of DEF at $50
    Short 1 DEF Feb 55 calls at 3
    Short 1 DEF Feb 45 puts at 2

    What is Mr. Simpson's maximum gain?

    (A) Unlimited
    (B) $600
    (C) $800
    (D) 1,000

42. Which of the following is not a bearish strategy?

    (A) A long 40 put and a short 35 put
    (B) Uncovered call writing
    (C) A long 80 call and a short 75 call
    (D) Protective put purchase

43. Gail purchased 2 WJI Aug 40 puts at 2 and sold 2 WJI Aug 50 puts at 6. What is Gail's breakeven point?

    (A) $38
    (B) $36
    (C) $44
    (D) $46

44. Which one of the following principal licenses is required to approve a customer account for options trading?

    (A) Series 4
    (B) Series 24
    (C) Series 53
    (D) Series 27

45. Marvin just purchased an ABC Sept 50 put at 4. In which of the following scenarios would Marvin lose his entire premium? At expiration, ABC stock is trading:

    I.   below its strike price
    II. above its strike price
    III. at its strike price

    (A) I only
    (B) II only
    (C) I and III only
    (D) II and III only

46. An investor is short 5 PFE June 40 puts. He can liquidate his position by entering which of the following transactions? Buy 5 PFE:

    (A) June 40 puts
    (B) Apr 40 puts
    (C) June 45 puts
    (D) Apr 45 puts

47. An investor buys a GHI Mar 25 call at 3. Two month later the investor exercises the call option. Two years later the investor sells 100 GHI stock at $50/share. Which two of the following are true?

    I.   The cost basis on GHI stock is $2,500
    II. The cost basis on GHI stock is $2,800
    III. The sales proceeds on GHI are $5,000
    IV   The sales proceeds on GHI are $4,700

    (A) I and III
    (B) I and IV
    (C) II and III
    (D) II and IV

48. Which of the following accurately describes an "Order Book Official"?

    (A) An exchange member whose function is to provide liquidity by making bids and offers for his account in the absence of public buy or sell orders
    (B) An exchange employee in charge of keeping a book of public limit orders on exchanges utilizing the market maker system
    (C) An exchange member whose function is to make markets and to keep the book of public orders
    (D) An agent on the exchange floor who executes the orders of public customers and other investors

49. An investor buys an XYZ Apr 40 call at 2.
    Three month later, the investor exercises the
    call option. Two years later the investor
    sells 100 XYZ stock at $37. Which two of
    the following are true?

    I.   The investor has a short-term capital
         loss of $500.
    II. The investor has a long-term capital loss
         of $500.
    III. The sales proceeds on XYZ stock are
         $3,700
    IV. The sales proceeds on XYZ are $3,500

    (A) I and III
    (B) I and IV
    (C) II and III
    (D) II and IV

50. Ronald buys 1 ABC June 65 call and sells I
    ABC Sept 70 call. What is the name of this
    strategy?

    (A) Vertical Spread
    (B) Straddle
    (C) Diagonal Spread
    (D) Horizontal Spread

OPTIONS EXPLANATIONS 5

1. **(C)**

Note that this is an "Except" question. All spreads (A & B) have limited risk, whether they are debit spreads, credit spreads, bull or bear spreads. Spread positions are designed to reduce risk.

Protective call purchases (D) involve the purchase of a call option to protect a short stock position. Normally, we think of short stock ('"selling short") as having unlimited risk. However, with a protective call, it involves the purchase of a call option. If the stock were to rise to infinity (theoretically), the short seller would not have to go out to the open market and purchase the stock. The short seller could exercise the call option, purchasing the stock at the exercise price, hence covering their short stock position.

A short combination consists of a short call and short put on the same security with either different strike prices, expiration dates, or both. Embedded in a short combination is a naked call option which lends the position to unlimited risk.

2. **(D)**

As a result of the two transactions, Tara realized a loss of $50. To determine the loss in dollars, we can apply the following formula:

Transaction	Debit or Credit
Bought 2 EBAY Sept 30 Puts at 4	-$800 debit
Sold 2 EBAY Sept 30 Puts at 3.75	+$750 credit
Loss or Net Debit = -$50	

3. **(D)**

A call option has intrinsic value or is in-the-money when the market price of the stock is above the exercise price of the call option. As a result, the XON Oct 75 calls have two points of intrinsic value. It is also important to note that we focus on the option series, not whether the investor is long or short.

4. **(A)**

The formula for determining the breakeven point of a put is the following:

Strike Price	- Premium	= Breakeven Point
40	-7	=33

The investor breaks even at $33/share. The investor could purchase ABC stock at $33/share in the market, and exercise his put, selling his ABC stock at $40. As a result of these two transactions, he would earn $7/share, recouping his $7 premium paid.

5. **(D)**

The purchase of 1 XYZ June 65 put would create a Bullish Vertical Spread, which consists of the purchase and sale of calls or puts on the same security, same expiration dates, and different strike prices. Since the question began by writing a put with a June expiration, we can eliminate Choices A and C since they contain Sept expiration dates. Since our choices can be narrowed down to B and D, we must purchase the put option with the lower strike price to create a bullish position, Choice D.

6. **(A)**

A stock dividend is treated in the same manner as an odd stock split. That is the number of shares per contract increases while the strike price decreases proportionally.

For example, Scott owns 1 DEF Nov 50 call. The company declares a 10% stock dividend. Scott still owns 1 contract, but now the contract size is 110 shares. (100 shares x 10% = 10 additional shares) To determine the adjusted price, use the following method:

<u>Aggregate exercise price</u> Adjusted number of shares	= Adjusted Exercise Price
<u>$5,000</u> 110 shares	= 45.45

The adjusted exercise price or strike price after the stock dividend is 45.45.

7. **(B)**

The two allocation methods a broker-dealer may be permitted to utilize are "random selection" and "oldest position" (technically, this is First-in, First-out). Allocating an assignment notice based upon the smallest or largest position is considered to be discriminatory, and therefore not permissible.

8. **(A)**

Foreign currencies trade on the Philadelphia Stock Exchange. While the Chicago Board Options Exchange (CBOE) is the largest options exchange, they do not trade foreign currency options. The interbank market is the largest market in the world for trading the underlying foreign currencies. And while C appears to be a viable choice, there is no such exchange as the Philadelphia Options Exchange.

9. **(C)**

The formula for determining the breakeven point of a call is the following:

Strike Price	+ Premium	= Breakeven Point
75	+3	= 78

Ed breaks even at $78/share. He could exercise his call options, purchasing XON stock at $75/share and then sell the stock in the market at $78. As a result of these two transactions, he would earn $3/share, recouping his $3 premium paid.

10. **(A)**

The Series 7 exam does not recognize U.S. dollar options, so Choices B and C can be eliminated. Always select a choice in terms of the foreign currency, not U.S. dollars. Since Trader Joe expects the British Pound to strengthen against the U.S. dollar, the purchase of call options on the U.S. dollar would position Joe to make a profit should he be correct.

11. **(B)**

On the Series 7 exam, all foreign currencies have a contract size of 10,000 with the exception of the Japanese Yen, which has a contract size of 1 million.

12. **(A)**

Debit spreads can be purchased in a cash account because the most the spread investor can lose is the net debit. Credit spreads cannot be purchased in a cash account. Choice A is an example of a credit spread since the option written would have a premium that is higher than the option that would be purchased.

13. **(D)**

Taleen has created a Protective Call Purchase. The formula for the breakeven of a protective call purchase is as follows:

Short Sale price	+ Premium of call option	= breakeven point
$65/share	- 5	= $60

Taleen would breakeven at $60/share. She is bearish on ABC stock, and at $60/share she would earn a profit of $5/share on the short sale, recouping the 5-point premium paid for the call options.

14. **(B)**

The position is a Protective Put Purchase, which consists of a long stock position and a long put(s). Bob is long 10 XYZ puts only as an insurance policy to protect against a decline in his long XYZ stock position. Bob's breakeven point can be determined as follows:

Purchase Price of Stock	+ Premium	= Breakeven Point/share
$50	+ 2	= $52

Bob needs XYZ stock to rise to $52/share to recoup the 2-point premium paid for the puts. So, at $52/share, the following would result: His XYZ stock, which was purchased at $50/share, is sold at $52/share resulting in a 2-point profit. The 2-point profit on the sale of the stock is offset against the 2-point premium paid for the put options. The result is no gain or loss.

15. **(B)**

Since the speculator expects the dollar to strengthen against the Swiss Franc, this translates to the speculator having a bearish view on the Swiss Franc. The purchase of puts and the sale of calls on the Swiss Franc would be consistent with this bearish view.

16. **(B)**

The premium of an option is composed of intrinsic value + time value. Prior to expiration, an option always has time value. An option may or may not have intrinsic value or money value. To determine if an option has intrinsic value, focus on the relationship between the exercise price and market price. A call option has intrinsic value when the exercise price is below the market price. A put option has intrinsic value when the exercise price is above the market price.

17. **(A)**

The formula for determining the breakeven point of a put is the following:

Strike Price	- Premium	= Breakeven Point
35	-5	=30

The investor breaks even at $30/share. If ABC stock traded $30/share, the writer would receive an assignment notice which would obligate him to purchase ABC stock at the strike price of $35/share. He would then own a stock at $35/share when the market price would be $30/share. This 5-point loss would be offset by the 5-point premium received, resulting in no profit or loss.

18. **(C)**

Mr. Halasi bought 10 DEF 80 puts for a premium of 3.50. The dollar amount of the premium can be calculated as follows:

Premium	X Number of contracts	X Contract Size	= $premium
3.50	X 10	X 100	= $3,500 (debit)

Since the puts expired worthless, the maximum loss would be the debit of $3,500.

19. **(A)**

If Scott only went short or wrote a July 80 call, he would be subject to unlimited risk. By also going long or purchasing the July 85 call, he has created a bearish vertical spread. By creating a bearish vertical spread, Scott has limited his maximum loss.

20. **(D)**

Choices A, B, and C are examples in which the investor would be considered covered for margin purposes. In this context, "covered means that there is no margin requirement on the sale of the call options. Choice D, is the correct answer since this is an Except question. The investor would not be considered covered since he owns a convertible bond, and has not yet tendered the bond for conversion.

21. **(B)**

MSFT put options are an example of a Class of options.

Let's start from the most basic terminology and get more specific as we progress.

- A "Type" consists of all call options or all put options, which divides the options universe into two groups.

- A "Class" consists of the same security, and the same type. An example of a class would be all MSFT put options. Another example of a class would be all IBM call options.

- A "Series" consists of the same class, same expiration date, and same strike price. You may think of a Series as being the most specific.

22. **(B)**

The first step in the process is being able to identify an odd stock split, which always ends with a ratio other than 1. Examples include 3 for 2, 4 for 3, 5 for 2, etc. In the case of a 5 for 2 stock split, Tom will receive five shares for every two shares that he owns.

Option contracts are also affected in that the exercise price decreases while the number of shares per contract increases proportionally. Note, the number of contracts remain unchanged.

In the example, Tom owns 1 ABC July 60 call. After the 5 for 2 split, he will now own 1 ABC July 24 call (2/5 x 60). Note the number of shares per contract is now 250 (5/2 x 100). Also note the aggregate exercise price remains unchanged at $6,000.

23. **(D)**

Marissa has created a Covered Put Writing strategy. We can determine the breakeven point of a Covered Put Writing strategy is as follows:

Short Sale price	+ Premium of put option	= breakeven point
$40/share	+ 3	= $43

Marissa would break even at $43/share. While she is bearish on PNO stock, if the position moved against her at $43/share she would have a loss on the short sale which would be equally offset against the 3-point premium received for writing the put option.

While this position has unlimited risk because of the short sale, it gives Marissa a higher breakeven point should the stock move against her (rise) in the short term.

24. **(B)**

Tina has created a Bullish Vertical Spread. We will begin by rewriting the position as follows:

Transactions	Premium
Purchased 2 ABC Aug 40 Calls	-6 (debit)
Sold 2 ABC Aug 50 Calls	+2 (credit)
Net debit = -4	

We can now apply the following formula to determine the breakeven point:

Strike Price of the dominant leg of the spread (leg with the higher premium)	+ Net Debit (note that we add the net amount for call spreads; if this was a put spread we would subtract the net amount)	= Breakeven Point
40	+ 4	= 44

So, Tina breaks even when ABC stock trades $44/share, which means she could exercise her 2 ABC Aug 40 calls, buying the stock at $40/share and then selling the stock in the market at $42/share. Tina would earn a 4-point profit, recouping her 4-point net debit paid for the spread.

25. **(B)**

Jack has created a Covered Call Writing strategy. Since Jack implemented this strategy in his cash account, he would be required to deposit 100% of the purchase price of the stock less the premium received. The full purchase price (100%) of the stock is $12,675. The premium received is $1,500. $12,675 - $1,500 = $11,175.

26. **(A)**

The Swiss Exporter will be receiving payment in U.S. dollars, which is not its preferred currency. The fear is that the U.S. dollar will weaken, or stated another way, the Swiss Franc will strengthen. The Swiss Exporter needs to assume bullish positions in the Swiss Franc, which would be to buy Swiss Franc calls and sell Swiss Franc puts.

27. **(D)**

The Registered Options Principal ("ROP") has approved the account for options trading based on current information supplied by the customer. The customer must now execute the agreement within 15 days of the ROP's approval, verifying that the information provided to the broker-dealer is accurate.

28. **(D)**

All three supervisory activities are responsibilities of the Registered Options Principal ("ROP"). All supervisory activities that involve options require review by an ROP (Series 4).

29. **(C)**

When an investor "exercises" an IBM call option, she is buying IBM stock at $135/share (strike price). Since this is a stock purchase, it follows a three day settlement convention (T+3).

Note, if the question instead read, "An investor *buys* an IBM Apr 135 call," this would be an options purchase, and would settle next business day (T+1).

30. **(C)**

Foreign currency options trade between the hours of 9:30am and 4pm EST on the Philadelphia Stock Exchange. This should not be confused with the Interbank Market in which major banks trade foreign currencies 24 hours, 7 days per week.

31. **(A)**

Julie earns a profit of $250 as follows:

Type of Transaction	Transaction	Premium
Opening Sale	Short 10 AMZN Aug 180 puts	+$3,000 (credit)
Closing Purchase	Long 10 AMZN Aug 180 puts	-$2,750 (debit)
+250 Profit		

32. **(C)**

Choice C is a bull spread. We need to determine which leg of each spread would have a higher premium. Even though premiums are not given, we can attribute a higher premium to the leg to the call option with:

- Lower strike price
- Longer expiration date

With Choice C, we can attribute a higher premium to the Sept 65 call because it has a lower strike price and a longer expiration date. Since this option is a "long" call or involves the purchase of a call, the spread is bullish.

33. **(D)**

Ryan has established a Protective call purchase.   Let's take a closer look at the position:

Transaction	Debit or Credit
Short sale of 1,000 EWZ	+$55,000 (credit)
Bought 10 EWZ Aug 60 calls	-$3,000 (debit)
+52,000 maximum potential gain	

Ryan's core position is the short sale. If EWZ stock declines to zero, he would earn $55,000 on the short sale less the $3,000 premium paid for the EWZ call options.

34. **(D)**

Since the speculator expects the dollar to weaken against the Euro, this translates to the speculator having a bullish view on the Euro. The purchase of calls and the sale of puts on the Euro would be consistent with this bullish view.

35. **(B)**

The purchase of combinations would be consistent with his expectation of trading over a wide range, in other words, an expectation of volatility. The purchase of a combination consists of buying a call and a put on the same security, with different expiration dates and/or strike prices. Similar in concept to a long straddle, combination buyers expect volatility.

36. **(D)**

Regular way settlement for options transactions (foreign currencies, equities, bonds, indices) are T+1 or trade date + one business day.

37. **(C)**

Two factors attribute to a higher premium:

- Put option with the higher strike price (the opposite would be true for call options)
- Longer expiration date

Since the Aug 20 puts have the longest expiration date and highest strike price, its premium would also command the largest premium in the marketplace.

38. **(A)**

The question reads: "Which of the following option strategies does NOT have limited loss potential?" In other words, which option strategy has unlimited loss potential?

Short call options have unlimited loss potential, as the underlying (i.e., security, currency, index) could theoretically rise to infinity. The writer (short) of the call would be obligated to sell the stock at the strike price. Since he does not own the underlying, he would first need to go out to the market and purchase the underlying at an infinite price.

39. **(B)**

Regular-way settlement on an equity transaction is the trade date + three business days (T+3). Which means the buyer of an equity security must purchase the stock prior to the ex-dividend date. In roman numerals I and IV, the investor is effective purchasing the stock prior to the ex-dividend date as follows:

- A call buyer that exercises his option the day prior to the ex-dividend date is purchasing the stock prior to the ex-dividend date

- IV. A put writer that is assigned an exercise notice the day before the ex-dividend date is obligated to purchase the stock prior to the ex-dividend date

40. **(C)**

The regulation T margin requirement is 100% on the purchase of options (both calls and puts). The purchase price is calculated as follows:

Premium	X Number of Contracts	X Contract Size	= $Premium
3	X 2	X 100	= $600

41. **(D)**

The three positions can be rearranged into two strategies as follows:

Covered Call Writing Strategy
Long 100 shares of DEF at $50
Short 1 DEF Feb 55 calls at 3
Maximum Gain = $800

Even though Mr. Simpson is long DEF stock, he does not have unlimited upside potential. He will only profit from $50 (the price he purchased the stock) to $55 as the stock would be called away from him above $55/share, plus the 3-point premium received for a total of $800.

Put Writing Strategy
Short 1 DEF Feb 45 puts at 2
Maximum gain = $200

The maximum gain for writing a put is the premium received of $200. In total, Mr. Simpson's maximum gain is $1,000 in total.

42. **(D)**

A Protective Put Purchase is a bullish position and consists of a long stock position and a long put. For example, an investor buys 100 GHI at $50/share and buys a GHI May 45 call at 2. This strategy is utilizing the long put as only as an insurance policy to protect against a decline in his long stock position in GHI.

The other three strategies are bearish for the following reasons:

- Long 40 put and a short 35 put (A) is a bearish strategy, as the higher premium would be attributed to the long 40 put since it has a higher exercise price than the 35 put.

- Uncovered call writing (B) is a bearish strategy, as it involves the sale of a naked or uncovered call option.

- Long 80 call and a short 75 call (C) is a bearish strategy, as the higher premium would be attributed to the 75 call since it has a lower exercise price than the 80 call.

43. **(D)**

Gail has created a Credit Put Spread. By buying 2 WJI Aug 40 Puts at 2 and selling 2 WJI Aug 50 Puts at 6, she has a net credit of 4 points. In other words, Gail received more money than has been paid out, establishing a net credit of 4 points.

To determine the breakeven point, utilize the following steps:

1. Determine the dominant leg of the spread; this is the put option with the higher premium. This is the Aug 50 puts.

2. Strike price from the dominant leg – net credit, 50 – 4 = 46

The breakeven is $46/share. At $46/share the Aug 40 puts that Claudia purchased are worthless. The Aug 50 puts have four points of intrinsic value and would be exercised against Claudia, creating a 4 point loss. The 4-point loss from the Aug 50 puts would be offset by the net credit that Claudia received by establishing the spread. Therefore, if WJI stock is trading at $46/share at expiration, Claudia does not make or lose money.

44. **(A)**

A Series 4 or Registered Options Principal is permitted to approve a customer account for options trading. Additionally, a Series 9-10 or General Securities Sales Supervisor is also permitted to approve customer accounts for options trading.

45. **(D)**

At expiration, a put option would expire worthless if the underlying security is above its strike price or (out-of-the-money) (II) or at its strike price (at-the-money) (III).

46. **(A)**

The investor initiated his position with an opening sale. To liquidate his existing position, he would need to engage in a closing transaction. Since he initially "sold" puts, he would now need to buy put options, which would require a "closing purchase".

Note: To liquidate the position, the investor had to engage in a closing purchase with the same number of option contracts in the same series - PFE June 40 Puts.

47. **(C)**

The investor has a cost basis of $2,800 on GHI stock as the exercise prices of $2,500 plus the premium of $300 are added together. When the investor sells the stock two years later, his sales proceeds are $5,000 or the price at which he actually sold GHI stock.

48. **(B)**

Choice B accurately describes the role of an Order Book Official as an exchange employee in charge of keeping a book of public limit orders on exchanges utilizing the market marker system. The other market participants are described as follows:

- Choice A – Market Maker
- Choice C – Specialist
- Choice D – Floor Broker

49. **(C)**

The investor has a long-term capital loss of $500 because his holding period began the day following exercising the call, and ended two years later on the sale date. A long-term capital loss (or gain) is one with a holding period of 12 months and one day or longer. His cost basis is the exercise price of $4,000 + $200 premium paid for a total of $4,200. His sales proceeds were $3,700 which produced a $500 long-term capital loss.

50. **(C)**

Ron has created a Diagonal spread, which consists of the purchase or sale calls, or puts on the same security with different expiration dates and exercise prices.

OPTIONS EXAM 6

1. Tim buys 2 DEF July 50 puts and sells 2 DEF July 55 puts. What is the name of this strategy?

   (A) Calendar Spread
   (B) Price Spread
   (C) Straddle
   (D) Diagonal Spread

2. Foreign currency options have which of the following exercise styles?

   (A) European
   (B) American
   (C) Foreign
   (D) Australian

3. Suzie purchased 1 OX Aug 30 put at 3 and sold 1 OX Aug 25 put at 2. At what price would the underlying stock need to trade for Suzie to break even?

   (A) $29
   (B) $27
   (C) $23
   (D) $25

4. Marissa goes long 1 T-bond Oct 99 call at 4.19. One week later, she liquidates her position at 5.17. What is Marissa's resulting profit?

   (A) $9,375
   (B) $937.50
   (C) $9,800
   (D) $980

5. An investor writes 1 DEF June 70 put. The addition of which of the following would create a Bearish Vertical spread? Buy 1 DEF:

   (A) Sept 75 put
   (B) June 75 put
   (C) Sept 70 put
   (D) June 65 put

6. Roy sells an XYZ Mar 45 put at 3 when the underlying stock is trading at $47.25. Which two of the following are correct?

   I. Intrinsic value is equal to 2.25 points.
   II. Time value is equal to .75 of a point.
   III. Intrinsic value is equal to zero points.
   IV. Time value is equal to 3 points.

   (A) I and II
   (B) I and IV
   (C) II and III
   (D) III and IV

7. Mike buys 1 XYZ Jan 65 put and sells I XYZ Apr 65 put. What is the name of this strategy?

   (A) Time Spread
   (B) Straddle
   (C) Price Spread
   (D) Diagonal Spread

8. Microsoft common stock has been halted from trading on the Nasdaq. Microsoft options are trading on the CBOE. Who is responsible for halting trading in the options?

   (A) FINRA
   (B) Microsoft
   (C) OCC
   (D) CBOE

9. An investor buys an HD May 35 call for 5 and also buys an HD May 30 put for 3. The stock rises to $41, and the put expires worthless. The investor exercises the call and sells the stock at the market. What is the resulting profit or loss?

   (A) $200 profit
   (B) $200 loss
   (C) $800 loss
   (D) $3,300 profit

10. Eddie is long 5 IBM June 135 calls. His goal is to maintain a moderately bullish position while reducing the overall cost of his long position in IBM calls. The addition of which of the following positions would best meet his objective?

    (A) Short 5 IBM June 130 calls
    (B) Short 5 IBM June 135 puts
    (C) Long 5 IBM June 135 calls
    (D) Short 5 IBM June 140 calls

11. Doug writes 1 XYZ Oct 50 put at 3. Doug's position would be considered covered under all of the following conditions EXCEPT:

    (A) short 100 shares of XYZ
    (B) $5,000 cash deposit in Doug's account
    (C) long 100 shares of XYZ
    (D) long 1 XYZ Oct 55 put

12. Which one of the following statements is true concerning the characteristics of listed options?

    (A) Premiums are determined by the OCC.
    (B) The investor chooses the exercise style.
    (C) All options have time value.
    (D) All options have intrinsic value.

13. Don buys 3 XYZ July 65 calls and sells 3 XYZ Aug 70 calls. What is the name of this strategy?

    (A) Vertical Spread
    (B) Straddle
    (C) Diagonal Spread
    (D) Horizontal Spread

14. A customer establishes the following position:

    Long 1 XOM Aug 75 call at 5
    Short 1 XOM Aug 80 call at 3
    Short 100 shares of XOM stock at $75

    What is the customer's maximum loss?

    (A) $7,700 loss
    (B) $7,500 loss
    (C) $7,200 loss
    (D) Unlimited loss

15. Bruce goes long 200 shares of XYZ stock at $40. He also goes long 2 XYZ Oct 35 puts at 2. At what price does XYZ stock need to trade for Bruce to earn a profit?

    (A) $42
    (B) $43
    (C) $37
    (D) $33

16. Stan buys 1 ABC Oct 65 put and sells 1 ABC Oct 70 put. Which two of the following are characteristics of this strategy?

    I.   Credit
    II. Debit
    III. Bullish
    IV. Bearish

    (A) I and III
    (B) I and IV
    (C) II and III
    (D) II and IV

17. An investor goes long an XYZ Nov 50 put and also goes short an XYZ Sept 50 put. This is an example of a:

    (A) diagonal spread
    (B) vertical spread
    (C) horizontal spread
    (D) combination

18. A customer sells short 500 XYZ at $60/share and also writes 5 XYZ Nov 60 puts at 3. The customer will break even when the underlying stock is trading at which of the following prices?

    (A) $57
    (B) $63
    (C) $45
    (D) $75

19. Which one of the four strategies has unlimited gain potential?

    (A) Short straddle
    (B) Long straddle
    (C) Covered call
    (D) Vertical spread

20. John Simpson sold short 500 shares of XYZ Corp at $80/share. He also wrote 5 XYZ Feb 70 puts at 3. What is his maximum potential loss?

   (A) Unlimited
   (B) $4,300
   (C) $3,700
   (D) $300

21. A customer buys 100 shares of HD common stock at $45 and also writes 1 HD June 50 call at 3. Which two of the following would be the correct way to mark the options order ticket?

   I.   Closing sale
   II. Opening sale
   III. Covered
   IV. Uncovered

   (A) I and III
   (B) I and IV
   (C) II and III
   (D) II and IV

22. An investor writes 1 XOM Sept 80 put at 2 when XOM is trading at $91. What is the investor's margin requirement?

   (A) $1,120
   (B) $1,310
   (C) $920
   (D) $1,110

23. The HD July 45 put options are an example of a:

   (A) type
   (B) series
   (C) strategy
   (D) class

24. Peter Leach is a portfolio manager of the New Era Telecommunications Fund. Which of the following would be best for hedging his portfolio? The:

   (A) purchase of broad-based index put options
   (B) sale of broad based index call options
   (C) purchase of narrow-based index put options
   (D) sale of narrow-based index call options

25. A customer would like to write 10 ABC Oct 40 puts in his cash account. Under which of the following circumstances is this permissible? In his account he:

   (A) purchases 10 ABC Oct 35 puts.
   (B) writes 10 ABC Oct 35 calls.
   (C) deposits $40,000 in cash.
   (D) sells short 1,000 shares of ABC stock.

26. Jon buys a Ford June 15 call option at 5.25. Jon has the right to exercise this option at any time prior to expiration. What style of exercise is this?

   (A) American Style
   (B) European Style
   (C) Bermuda Style
   (D) North American Style

27. An investor writes 10 ABC Nov 45 puts at 3. One month later, the investor receives an assignment notice when the stock is trading at $41. After fulfilling his obligation, the investor's cost basis on the stock is:

   (A) $45,000
   (B) $42,000
   (C) $41,000
   (D) $48,000

28. Kent goes long 10 TYU Feb 70 puts at 6. What is Kent's maximum potential gain?

   (A) $6,400
   (B) $64,000
   (C) $7,000
   (D) $70,000

29. Peter goes long 1 XDC (Canadian Dollar) May 100 call option for a premium of 3.25. What is Peter's maximum loss?

   (A) $3,250
   (B) $325
   (C) Unlimited
   (D) $32,500

30. In his margin account, an investor purchases 1 ABC May 60 put at 5. How much must the investor deposit?

   (A) $250
   (B) $500
   (C) $1,000
   (D) $2,000

31. Phil writes 1 KLM Oct 45 straddle at 7.25. What is Phil's maximum gain?

   (A) $725
   (B) Unlimited
   (C) $1,450
   (D) $5,225

32. An investor writes 1 DEF Apr 55 call at 6 when DEF stock is trading at $56/share. What is the investor's margin requirement?

   (A) $1,720
   (B) $1,160
   (C) $600
   (D) $2,300

33. Terry writes an uncovered XON Dec 45 put at 3. Which two of the following best describe this strategy?

   I.   Bullish strategy
   II.   Bearish strategy
   III. Limited loss potential
   IV.   Unlimited loss potential

   (A) I and III
   (B) I and IV
   (C) II and III
   (D) II and IV

34. On March 8, 2008 Dave bought 1 XON Oct 50 LEAP at 9. On July, 8, 2010, the XON option expires worthless. For tax purposes, Dave has a $900:

   (A) long-term capital loss.
   (B) long-term ordinary loss.
   (C) short-term capital loss.
   (D) short-term ordinary loss.

35. Raj buys 100 shares of HD at $30 and sells an HD Nov 35 call for 6. At expiration, what price would HD stock need to trade for Raj to break even?

   (A) $36
   (B) $24
   (C) $29
   (D) $41

36. The dollar value of a basis point for T-bill options is:

   (A) $100
   (B) $25
   (C) $10
   (D) $2.50

37. Jack goes long 1 SPX (S&P 500 Index) June 245 call for a premium of 4.15. What is Jack's maximum potential loss?

   (A) $4,150
   (B) Unlimited
   (C) $415
   (D) $2,450

38. Bosco buys 1 MNO May 40 put at 3 and also buys 1 MNO May 40 call at 3. At what price will Bosco earn a profit?

   (A) $34
   (B) $46
   (C) $33
   (D) $45

39. Jim sold a FIG Dec 65 call at 6. What is Jim's maximum potential gain?

    (A) $5,900
    (B) $600
    (C) Unlimited
    (D) $7,100

40. Which two of the following are valid reasons as to why an investor may purchase a put option?

    I. Protect a short position
    II. Protect a long position
    III. To speculate that the underlying stock will decline
    IV. To speculate that the underlying stock will increase

    (A) I and III
    (B) I and IV
    (C) II and III
    (D) II and IV

41. Bobby buys 1 LNP Mar 45 put at 3 and also buys 1 LNP Mar 50 call at 4.50. At which of the following prices will Bobby break even?

    I. $57.50
    II. $54.50
    III. $37.50
    IV. $42

    (A) I and III
    (B) I and IV
    (C) II and III
    (D) II and IV

42. What is the contract size for Japanese Yen (¥) options?

    (A) 100 ¥
    (B) 1,000 ¥
    (C) 10,000 ¥
    (D) 1,000,000 ¥

43. Vincent purchases a DEF May 55 put for $400 when the underlying stock is trading at $57. What is the time value of the put option?

    (A) $400
    (B) -$200
    (C) $200
    (D) $0

44. On March 10, 2009 an investor purchased 500 shares of CVS stock at $30 and also wrote 5 CVS Sept 35 calls at 3. On Sept 15, 2009 CVS stock trades at $37/share and the calls are exercised. What are the tax consequences?

    (A) $4,000 short-term capital gain
    (B) $4,000 long-term capital gain
    (C) $2,500 short-term capital gain
    (D) $2,500 long-term capital gain

45. A member firm would like to embark on a marketing campaign in order to increase its revenue from options trading. A marketing campaign utilizing which of the following mediums would meet the definition of an advertisement?

    I. Radio
    II. Television
    III. Newspaper
    IV. Magazine

    (A) I and II only
    (B) II and III only
    (C) III and IV only
    (D) I, II, III, IV

46. Kimberly purchased ABC stock at $20 six months ago. Currently the stock is trading at $32/share. While Kimberly is bullish on ABC stock over the long-term, she believes the stock will decline sharply over the next three months. As her registered rep, which of the following strategies would you recommend to her?

 (A) Buy puts on ABC stock
 (B) Write calls against ABC stock
 (C) Liquidate her entire position, and repurchase the stock after the sharp decline
 (D) Place a sell-stop order on ABC stock

47. Which two of the following can be grouped together in determining position limits?

 I.   Long calls
 II. Short calls
 III. Long puts
 IV. Short puts

 (A) I and II
 (B) I and III
 (C) II and III
 (D) III and IV

48. An investor wrote 1 ABC Feb 50 Call at 6. Under which two of the following conditions would his position be considered covered?

 I.   Bank escrow receipt for 100 shares of ABC stock
 II. Owns 1 ABC Feb 55 call
 III. Short 1 ABC Feb 50 put
 IV. Owns an ABC convertible bond that allows for conversion into 100 shares

 (A) I and III
 (B) I and IV
 (C) II and III
 (D) II and IV

49. An investor writes 1 XOM Sept 80 put at 3 when XOM is trading at $77/share. What is the investor's margin requirement?

 (A) $1,840
 (B) $1,070
 (C) $2,140
 (D) $1,370

50. The premium of a T-bill option is 1.25. This translates to a price of:

 (A) $3,125
 (B) $13,500
 (C) $312.50
 (D) $1,350

OPTIONS EXPLANATIONS 6

1. (B)

Tim has created a Price Spread, which consists of the purchase and sale of either calls or puts on the same security, same expiration dates, but different strike prices.

2. (A)

Foreign currencies have a European style exercise, which only allows the option holder to exercise his option at one specific point in time, usually the day prior to expiration. This should not be confused with trading, liquidating, or selling a position which is permitted each day during normal trading hours.

3. (A)

Suzie has created a Debit Vertical Put Spread. By buying an OX Aug 30 Put at 3 and selling an OX Aug 25 Put at 2, she has a net debit of 1 point. In other words, Suzie paid out more money than she received, establishing a net debit of 1point.

We can determine the breakeven point as follows:

Strike Price from dominant leg	- Net amount	= Breakeven point

The dominant leg is the put option with the higher premium; this is the OX Aug 30 put option. The net amount is the net debit of 1 point.

30	- 1	= $29

The breakeven point is is $29/share. At $29/share the Aug 30 put that Suzie purchased has 1 point of intrinsic value. She could purchase OX stock in the market (at $29) and exercise the Aug 30 put, selling OX stock for a 1 point profit. The 1 point profit would be offset by the net debit that Suzie paid by establishing the spread. Therefore, if OX stock is trading at $29/share at expiration, Suzie does not make or lose money.

4. (B)

Marissa earned a profit of $937.50. It is important to remember that T-bond options are quoted as a percentage of par + 1/32. Par value is equal to $100,000. The value of 1/32 = $31.25. ($1,000/32 = $31.25). Now let's walk through the steps to see how Marissa earned a profit:

Sales Proceeds	Percentage of Par	+ 1/32
Short 1 T-bond Oct 99 call at 5.17	5% X $100,000	+ (17 X $31.25)
	$5,000	+ $531.25
Sales Proceeds = $5,531.25		

Cost Basis	Percentage of Par	+ 1/32
Long 1 T-bond Oct 99 call at 4.19	4% X $100,000	+ (19 X 31.25)
	$4,000	+ $593.75
Cost Basis = $4,593.75		

Sales Proceeds	- Cost Basis	= Profit (or loss)
$5,531.25	-$4,593.75	= $937.50

5. **(B)**

A bearish vertical spread utilizing puts is established by purchasing the put with the higher strike price and writing (selling) the put with the lower strike price. Since the question begins with the investor writing 1 DEF June 70 put, two choices containing expiration dates of Sept can be eliminated. That is because vertical spreads have the same expiration dates with different strike prices.

6. **(D)**

A put option has intrinsic value or is in-the-money when the strike price is above the market price of the underlying stock. As a result, the XYZ mar 45 puts have zero intrinsic value or are out-of-the-money. Once we are able to determine that the put option has zero intrinsic value, the remaining or entire premium is composed of time value.

7. **(A)**

Mike has created a Horizontal Spread, which consists of the purchase and sale of either puts or calls on the same security, same strike prices, but different expiration dates.

8. **(D)**

Since Microsoft ("MSFT") options trade on the CBOE, it is the responsibility of the CBOE to halt trading in MSFT options.

9. **(B)**

The resulting loss is $200. We can determine the amount of the loss as follows:

Transaction	Debit or Credit
Bought 1 HD May 35 call	-$500 debit
Bought 1 HD May 30 put	-$300 debit
Exercise of call	-$3,500 debit
Sale of stock	+$4,100 credit
Result = -$200 loss	

10. **(D)**

By going short 5 IBM June 140 calls, Eddie could create a Bullish Vertical spread. He maintains a moderately bullish position by being long the call options with the lower strike price. He has also reduced his maximum loss by establishing a net debit which would be substantially lower than the debit for just holding 5 IBM June 135 calls.

11. **(C)**

Covered in this context does not imply safety. Covered means covered for margin purposes whereby there is no additional margin deposit on the on the XYZ Oct 50 put that Doug has written for $300. Since this is an except question, we will first go through all the choices in which Doug would be covered, and we will finish with the choice in which Doug would not be considered covered

- Choice A – Short 100 shares of XYZ; a margin requirement of 50% applies to the short stock position only; the combined position would not create any additional risk compared to just a short sale XYZ stock, therefore no margin requirement is required on the writing of an XYZ Oct 50 put;

- Choice B - $5,000 cash deposit in Doug's account; cash equivalent to the aggregate exercise price of $5,000 should Doug receive an assignment notice;

- Choice C – Long 100 shares of XYZ; two bullish positions would exist, posing two separate margin requirements

- Choice D – Long 1 XYZ Oct 55 put; the purchase of a put with a higher strike price would create a position with a net debit; the margin requirement would be 100% of the net debit.

12. **(C)**

Prior to expiration, all options have time value. An option may or may not have intrinsic value. A call option has intrinsic value if the market price of the underlying stock is above the exercise price. A put option has intrinsic value if the exercise price is above the market price of the underlying stock.

The Options Clearing Corporation ("OCC') issues and guarantees all option contracts. The features that are standardized on an option contract include: underlying security, strike price, and expiration date. Premiums are determined by the forces of supply and demand (market price). The investor does not chose the exercise style as that feature is also set by the OCC.

13. **(C)**

Don has created a Diagonal spread, which consists of the purchase and sale of either calls or puts on the same security with different expiration dates and strike prices.

14. **(D)**

The three positions can be rearranged into two strategies as follows:

Bullish Vertical Spread
Long 1 XOM Aug 75 call at 5
Short 1 XOM Aug 80 call at 3
Maximum loss = $200

The bullish vertical spread has a maximum loss that is limited to the net debit of $200.

Short sale
Short 100 shares of XOM stock at $75
Maximum loss = unlimited

The short sale has unlimited loss potential. Overall, the customer's maximum loss is unlimited due to the short stock position.

15. **(B)**

The position is a Protective Put Purchase, which consists of a long stock position and a long put(s). Bruce is long 2 XYZ puts only as an insurance policy to protect against a decline in his long XYZ stock position.

While the question asks you to solve for a profit, we first need to determine the breakeven point. The breakeven point can be determined as follows:

Purchase Price of stock	+ Put Premium	= Breakeven Point
$40	+ 2	= $42

While Bruce needs XYZ stock to trade $42/share to breakeven, he will need the stock to increase above $42/share to earn a profit. The only choice above $42/share is choice B, $43. At $43/share, Bruce will earn a 1 point profit.

16. **(A)**

Stan has created a Bullish Vertical Credit Put Spread. We will begin by rewriting the position as follows:

Transactions
Bought 1 ABC Oct 65 put
Sold 1 ABC Oct 70 put (dominant position)

Even though premiums are not given in the question, the put option with the higher strike would have a larger premium, given the same expiration dates. We can now focus our attention on the put option with the higher premium. Since Stan has sold the ABC Oct 70 put, he would have a net credit. In addition, the sale of the Oct 70 put would also be bullish.

17. **(C)**

The investor has created a Horizontal Spread, which consists of the purchase and sale of either calls or puts on the same security, same strike prices, but different expiration dates.

18. **(B)**

The customer has created a Covered Put Writing strategy. The formula for the breakeven point of a Covered Put Writing strategy is as follows:

Short Sale price	+ Premium of put option	= breakeven point
$60/share	+ 3	= $63

The customer would breakeven at $63/share. While the customer is bearish on XYZ stock, if the position moved against him, at $63/share he would have a loss on the short sale which would be offset against the 3-point premium received for writing the put option. While this position has unlimited risk because of the short sale, it gives the customer a higher breakeven point should the stock move against him (rise) in the short term.

19. **(B)**

A long straddle has unlimited gain potential. It consists of the purchase of a call and put on the same security, same expiration dates, and strike prices. A straddle buyer has unlimited gain potential because a long call option is embedded in his position.

20. **(A)**

The customer has created a Covered Put Writing strategy. Covered in this context does not imply safety. It means covered for margin purposes whereby there is no additional margin requirement deposit on the sale of the 5 XYZ Feb 70 puts that John has written for a premium of 3. Theoretically, the short sale of 500 shares of XYZ Corp has unlimited risk. The sale of 5 XYZ Feb 70 puts does not offer John any protection should XYZ stock rise sharply.

21. **(C)**

Since the customer "initiated" the position with the sale of 1 HD June 50 call, the ticket should be marked as an "opening sale". In addition, the customer has established a Covered Call Writing Strategy. The Covered Call Writer owns (hence covered) the underlying stock. If the call is exercised by the buyer (holder), the covered call writer will sell the stock that he already owns at the strike price. So, the order ticket should be marked "covered".

22. **(D)**

The margin requirement for writing naked or uncovered options is the greater of the Basic Margin Requirement and the Minimum Margin Requirement. Let us review both margin requirements here:

Basic Margin Requirement			
Premium	+ (20% X current market value of the underlying stock)	- Out-of-money amount	= Basic Margin Requirement
$200	$1,820	- $1,100	$920

Minimum Margin Requirement		
Premium	+ (10% X current market value of the underlying stock)	= Minimum Margin Requirement
$200	+ $910	= $1,110

The greater of the Basic and Minimum Margin Requirement is $1,110.

23. **(B)**

Let us start by first defining Type, Class, and Series. A type divides the options universe into calls and puts. An example of a type includes all calls or all puts. A class consists of the same type and same security. An example of a class would be all calls on IBM or all puts on Home Depot. A series consists of the same security (HD), same expiration date (July), same strike price (45), and same type (put). So, the HD July 45 puts are an example of a series. You may think of a series as the most specific of the terms: type, class, and series.

24. **(C)**

Since Peter manages a sector fund, he could properly hedge this position by utilizing narrow-based index options that focus on the telecommunications sector. We can narrow the two choices down to C and D. However, the purchase of puts would be the much better choice as this would protect the portfolio from the strike price of the puts down to zero. The sale of call options would only offer protection limited to the premium received from the sale of the calls.

25. (C)

The customer would be able to write the 10 ABC Oct 40 puts in his cash account if he deposited $40,000 cash. The $40,000 would be cash equal to the aggregate exercise price should the customer receive an assignment notice. The other choices would not allow the investor to write the put options in his cash account for the following reasons:

Choice A – the purchase of puts with a lower strike price would result in a credit spread; credit spreads can only be established in a margin account.

Choice B – the investor would be creating a short straddle which involves unlimited risk as a result of the naked or uncovered calls embedded in the position; this is only permissible in a margin account.

Choice D – Short sales are only permitted in a margin account.

26. (A)

All equity options are American Style Exercise. This means that the holder (buyer) of a put or call has the right to exercise the option any time prior to expiration. This feature allows for maximum flexibility as opposed to a European Style Exercise which can only be exercised at one specific time prior to expiration, usually the last trading day prior to expiration. There is no such exercise style as North American. While a Bermuda exercise style does exist, it is not tested on the Series 7 exam.

27. (B)

Since the investor wrote 10 ABC Nov 45 puts at 3, his assignment notice translates to an obligation to buy 1,000 shares (10 contracts) of ABC at $45/share (exercise price). The cost basis is calculated as follows:

$Aggregate exercise price	- $Premium	= Cost basis
$45,000	- $3,000	= $42,000

The premium received (credit) is subtracted from the aggregate exercise price to determine the investor's cost basis because it reduces the investor's overall cost.

28. (B)

The put buyer's maximum gain is can be determined as follows:

Aggregate Exercise Price	-	Premium	= Maximum Gain
$70,000	-	$6,000	= $64,000

As the buyer of a put, Kent's maximum potential gain would be realized if the stock declined to zero. If TYU declines to zero, Kent could buy the stock at $0/share, and exercise his put, putting or selling the stock to the writer at the aggregate exercise price of $70,000. Kent's profit would be $70,000 less the $6,000 premium paid for the put options.

29. (B)

As with the purchase of any call or put option, the maximum loss to the buyer is the premium paid. The premium can be calculated as follows:

Premium	X Contract Size	X Number of Contracts	= $Can Aggregate Cost
.0325	X 10,000	X 1	$325

Note we first must move the decimal point on the premium TWO places to the left. Additionally, the contract size of the Canadian Dollar is 10,000. With only one exception, all other foreign currencies tested on the Series 7 exam, we move the decimal point on the premium TWO places to the left, and the contract sizes are 10,000. The one exception is the Japanese Yen in which the decimal point on the premium is moved four places to the left, and the contract size is 1 million.

30. **(B)**

As with the purchase of any call or put option, the premium is calculated as follows:

Premium	X Contract Size	X Number of Contracts	= $Aggregate Cost
5	X 100	X 1	$500

The Regulation T margin requirement is 100% of the premium paid or $500, regardless as to whether this is purchased in a cash or margin account.

31. **(A)**

The maximum gain is limited to the premium received which can be determined as follows:

Premium	X Number of Contracts	X Contract Size	= Maximum Gain
7.25	X 1	X 100	= $725

32. **(A)**

The margin requirement for writing naked or uncovered options is the greater of the Basic Margin Requirement or the Minimum Margin Requirement. Let's review both margin requirements here:

Basic Margin Requirement			
Premium	+ (20% X current market value of the underlying stock)	- Out-of-the-money amount	= Basis Margin Requirement
$600	+ $1,120	- 0	= $1,720

Minimum Margin Requirement		
Premium	+ (10% X current market value of the underlying stock)	= Basis Margin Requirement
$600	+ $560	= $1,160

The greater of the Basic and Minimum Requirement is $1,720.

33. **(A)**

The Put Writer is bullish, as he could receive an assignment notice, and therefore be obligated to purchase the stock at the strike price. His maximum potential loss would be the price he was assigned the stock less the premium received. The put writer's maximum loss can be expressed as follows:

Strike Price	-Premium	= Maximum loss

The maximum loss would be realized if the underlying security declined to zero.

34. **(A)**

Dave realized a long-term capital loss. The loss is considered long term because the date the LEAP was purchased and the date that it expired exceeded 12-months. It is also a capital loss as LEAPS (and all other securities) are capital assets and therefore subject to either capital gains or capital losses.

35. **(B)**

Raj has created a Covered Call Writing strategy. The formula for the breakeven point can be determined as follows:

Stock Price	- Premium	= Breakeven Point
$30	- 6	= $24

Raj would break even at $24/share. While he is bullish on HD stock, if the position moved against him, at $24/share, he would have a loss on the long stock position which would be equally offset against the 6-point premium received for writing the call option.

36. **(B)**

The T-Bill option is based upon a 13-week T-Bill with a $1 million face value. The value of a basis point is $1/100^{th}$ of 1%, expressed in decimal form as .0001. We can determine the dollar value by using the following formula:

Value of a Basis Point	X Contract Size (or face value)	X 25% (13-week T-Bill)	= $Value of a Basis Point
.0001	X 1,000,000	X .25	= $25

37. **(C)**

The maximum loss is the premium paid or debit of $415 and is calculated as follows:

Premium	X Contract Size	X Number of Contracts	= $Premium
4.15	X 100	X 1	= $415

38. **(C)**

You should be able to identify the position as a Long Straddle. The straddle buyer is long both a call and a put on the same security, same expiration dates, and same strike prices.

To determine where Bosco will earn a profit, we first need to determine the breakeven points. He will earn a profit if MNO stock trades above or below the breakeven points. A Straddle has two breakeven points which can be determined as follows:

Strike Price of Put	- Total Premium	= Downside Breakeven Point
40	- 6	= 34

Strike Price of Call	+ Total Premium	= Upside Breakeven Point
40	+ 6	= 46

Since Bosco will break even at $46/share and $34/share, he will earn a profit if MNO stock trades above $46 or below $34. The only choice (C) which is below the breakeven point is $33. Note there are no choices above $46.

39. **(B)**

The maximum gain is the premium received or credit of $600. It is calculated as follows:

Premium	X Contract Size	X Number of Contracts	= $Premium
6	X 100	X 1	= $600

40. **(C)**

The purchase of a put option can be either to:

- Protect or hedge a long position
  A Protective Put Purchase is a strategy whereby the investor goes long the stock, and purchases a put option to protect the long position;

- Speculate that the underlying stock will decline
  The investor is bearish and will profit from a decline in the underlying stock

41. **(A)**

Bobby has purchased a Combination. As a combination buyer, Bobby is long both a call and a put on the same security with different expiration dates or strike prices or both. A Combination buyer always has two breakeven points, calculated in the following manner:

Strike Price of Call Option	+ Total Premium	= Upside Breakeven Point
50	+ 7.50	= 57.50

Strike Price of Put Option	- Total Premium	= Downside Breakeven Point
45	- 7.50	= 37.50

It is important to add that a combination buyer expects "volatility". So if asked, Bobby would state the following: "Between now and expiration of the options, I expect LNP stock to trade above $57.50/share or below $37.50/share.

42. **(D)**

The contract size for the Japanese Yen option is 1,000,000. All other Foreign Currencies on the Series 7 exam have a contract size of 10,000.

43. **(A)**

The following method determines the Time Value of an option:

Option Premium	- Intrinsic Value	= Time Value

First we need to determine if the option has an intrinsic value or money value. A put option is in-the-money if the exercise price or strike price is above the market price of the underlying stock. Since the exercise price is below the market price, the option has zero intrinsic value (there is no such thing as negative intrinsic value). Let's go back to our example:

Option Premium	- Intrinsic Value	= Time Value
$400	- 0	=$400

The key is to always determine whether or not an option has intrinsic value or money value first before attempting to determine if an option has time value. Whatever amount remains is the time value.

44. **(A)**

We can determine whether the investor has a capital gain or loss by applying the following formula:

Sales Proceeds	-	Cost Basis	= Capital Gain (or loss)
Strike price of call + premium	-	Purchase price of stock	= Capital Gain (or loss)
$19,000	-	$15,000	= $4,000 Capital Gain

The result is a short-term capital gain of $4,000 since the holding period does not exceed 12 months.

45. **(D)**

An advertisement is any written form of communication in which the broker-dealer cannot control the audience that is viewing, listening to, or reading the communication. While a target market exists for radio, television, newspapers, and magazines, the audience that is viewing, listening to, or reading the communication cannot be controlled.

Option Advertisements are of particular concern to FINRA in that they are a complex product, and the broker-dealer cannot control the audience that is viewing the communication. As a result, FINRA requires options advertisements to be submitted to their Advertising Regulations Department ten (10) days prior to use.

46. **(A)**

The purchase of puts on ABC stock would create a Protective Put Purchase. Kimberly would utilize the long puts as only an insurance policy to protect against a decline in her long ABC stock position. In a worst case scenario, ABC stock declines to $0/share, and Kimberly exercises her put option and sells ABC stock at the strike price of the put option. For example, if the strike price of the ABC put is 25, Kimberly would sell her ABC stock at the strike price of $25/share, not the market price of $0/share.

47. **(C)**

Position limits apply to options on the same side of the market, summarized as follows:

Bullish Side of Market	**Bearish Side of Market**
Long Calls	Short Calls
Short Puts	Long Puts

48. **(B)**

The investor would be considered covered as long as he does not have to go out to the open market to purchase ABC stock in order to meet his obligation. A bank escrow receipt for 100 shares of ABC is the equivalent of owning 100 shares in his brokerage account. Additionally, the owner of a convertible bond that allows for conversion into 100 shares of ABC stock would also be covered. In the event of an assignment notice, the investor could simply convert his bond into 100 shares of stock that could be delivered.

49. **(A)**

The margin requirement for writing an uncovered option is the greater of the Basic Margin Requirement or Minimum Margin Requirement. Let's review both margin requirements here:

Basic Margin Requirement			
Premium	+ (20% X current market value of the underlying stock)	- Out-of-the-money amount	= Basis Margin Requirement
$300	+ $1,540	- 0	= $1,840

Minimum Margin Requirement		
Premium	+ (10% X current market value of the underlying stock)	= Basis Margin Requirement
$300	+ $770	= $1,070

The greater of the Basic and Minimum Requirement is $1,840.

50. **(A)**

The T-Bill option is based upon a 13-week T-Bill with a $1 million face value. The premium is expressed as a discounted yield since T-Bills are discounted securities. A premium of 1.25 is 1.25% or .0125. We can determine the dollar value by using the following formula:

Value of a Basis Point	X Contract Size (or face value)	X 25% (13-week T-Bill)	= $Value of a Basis Point
.0125	X 1,000,000	X .25	= $3,125

OPTIONS EXAM 7

1. Which of the following positions cannot be held in a cash account?

   (A) Writing puts secured by cash equivalent to the aggregate exercise price
   (B) Writing calls secured by cash equivalent to the aggregate exercise price
   (C) Debit diagonal call spread
   (D) Debit vertical put spread

2. A customer of E-Brokerage Corp sells short 500 shares of XOM at $75 and also writes 5 XOM Sept 80 puts at 3. What is the customer's margin requirement?

   (A) $37,500
   (B) $36,000
   (C) $18,750
   (D) $17,250

3. A customer goes long a BKR Apr 35 put at 7. Shortly thereafter, the customer decides to exercise his option when the common stock is trading at $32/share. Which two of the following correctly reflect the tax consequences?

   I. $300 capital gain
   II. $400 capital loss
   III. $3,500 sales proceeds
   IV. $2,800 sales proceeds

   (A) I and III
   (B) I and IV
   (C) II and III
   (D) II and IV

4. Which two of the following series would establish a short straddle?

   I.   Write 1 QRS Feb 65 call
   II. Buy 1 QRS Feb 65 call
   III. Write 1 QRS Feb 65 put
   IV. Write 1 QRS Feb 70 put

   (A) I and III
   (B) I and IV
   (C) II and III
   (D) II and IV

5. On February 8, 2010 Trader Matt is contemplating the purchase of put options on LTN stock. Which one of the following options would have the largest premium?

   (A) June 85 puts
   (B) June 90 puts
   (C) June 80 puts
   (D) June 75 puts

6. Stephen is bullish on LMT, which is trading at $40/share. He intends to invest $12,000. Which of the following is the best reason why he may purchase 3 LMT call options instead of buying 300 shares of LMT stock?

   (A) Increased leverage
   (B) Less risk
   (C) Lower transaction costs
   (D) Smaller cash commitment

7. Which of the following characteristics would be applicable to the buyer of a put?

   I.   Limited risk
   II. Protect a long position
   III. Use of leverage
   IV. Protect a short position

   (A) I only
   (B) I and III only
   (C) I, II, and III only
   (D) I, III, and IV only

8. An investor writes a T-Note Dec 98 straddle for a total premium of 5.13. At which two of the following prices would the investor break even?

   I.   103.13
   II. 92.87
   III. 103.41
   IV. 92.19

   (A) I and II
   (B) I and IV
   (C) II and III
   (D) III and IV

9. On September 9, 2010, Gary sold 1 SID Feb 55 call at 6. On January, 6, 2011, the SID option expires worthless. For tax purposes, Gary has a $600 a short term capital:

(A) loss in 2011.
(B) loss in 2010.
(C) gain in 2011.
(D) gain in 2010.

10. A customer wants to liquidate his short position. This transaction is considered:

(A) an opening purchase.
(B) a closing purchase.
(C) an opening sale.
(D) a closing sale.

11. Trader Mike goes long 5 ONM Mar 65 puts at 3. Where does the underlying stock need to trade for Mike to make a profit?

(A) $62
(B) $61.25
(C) $70.25
(D) $68.25

12. A customer goes long a Swiss Franc Dec 55 put and short a Swiss Franc Dec 57 put. This customer has established a:

(A) combination
(B) hedge
(C) bull spread
(D) bear spread

13. Carol sells short 1,000 ABC at $50, and goes long 10 ABC Dec 55 calls at 3. The following day, the stock jumps to $60 on very positive news. Carol takes immediate action by exercising the calls and covering her short position when the stock is trading at $52/per share. What is her resulting loss?

(A) $3,000
(B) $8,000
(C) $13,000
(D) $10,000

14. Pat buys 5 ABC June 50 calls at 5 and also sells 5 ABC June 55 calls at 2. In which of the following scenarios would Pat earn a profit?

(A) Spread narrows
(B) Spread widens
(C) Volatility increases
(D) Volatility decreases

15. An investor writes a Canadian Dollar Sept 155 put at 6.25. At the time of the sale, the Canadian Dollar is trading at 153.25. What are the investor's total sales proceeds received?

(A) $800
(B) $625
(C) $15,325
(D) $15,500

16. Danny purchased 1 DEF Apr 60 call at 7 and sold 1 DEF Apr 70 call at 4. What is his maximum potential gain?

(A) Unlimited
(B) $700
(C) $1,000
(D) $300

17. Which option strategy carries the greatest risk?

(A) Writing uncovered calls
(B) Writing uncovered puts
(C) Buying calls
(D) Buying puts

18. Pam buys 1 XYZ June 65 call and sells 1 XYZ Sept 65 call. What is the name of this strategy?

(A) Diagonal Spread
(B) Horizontal Spread
(C) Vertical Spread
(D) Straddle

19. Dave buys 10 PFE June 65 calls and also buys 10 PFE June 60 puts. What is the name of this strategy?

    (A) Straddle
    (B) Neutral Spread
    (C) Combination
    (D) Vertical Spread

20. An investor sells short 1,000 XYZ at $50/share, and also writes 10 XYZ July 45 puts at 3. What is the investor's cash deposit?

    (A) $25,000
    (B) $53,000
    (C) $28,000
    (D) $22,000

21. Sally goes long 1 XYZ Sept 30 call at 5, and long 1 XYZ Sept 30 put at 4.5. What is her maximum potential loss?

    (A) $950
    (B) $50
    (C) $500
    (D) $450

22. Which of the following is an example of a short straddle? Short 1 ABC June 80 call and short 1:

    (A) ABC June 80 put
    (B) XYZ June 80 put
    (C) ABC June 75 put
    (D) ABC July 80 put

23. A debit vertical put spread has which two of the following characteristics?

    I.   Unlimited risk
    II. Limited risk
    III. Bearish
    IV. Bullish

    (A) I and III
    (B) I and IV
    (C) II and III
    (D) II and IV

24. Which of the following is TRUE regarding the receipt of an assignment notice by the writer of a put option? The writer:

    (A) has an obligation to sell
    (B) has an obligation to buy
    (C) right to sell
    (D) right to buy

25. Ron buys 300 shares of DEF at $40/share. He also buys 3 DEF July 40 puts at 5. At what price does DEF stock need to trade for Ron to break even?

    (A) $45
    (B) $55
    (C) $35
    (D) $25

26. Which two of the following strategies has unlimited risk?

    I.   Put writer who is short the underlying stock
    II. Put writer who has cash in his account equal to the aggregate strike price
    III. Call writer who is long the underlying stock
    IV. Call writer who has written the equivalent number of puts on the same security

    (A) I and II
    (B) I and IV
    (C) II and III
    (D) II and IV

27. Which of the following positions cannot be held in a cash account? Long:

    (A) 1 XOM call and short 100 shares of XOM stock
    (B) 1 XOM put
    (C) 1 XOM straddle
    (D) 100 shares of XOM stock and short 1 XOM call

28. An investor buys an XYZ May 55 put for 5 and also writes an XYZ May 50 put for 3. How can this spread be described?

    (A) Bullish debit spread
    (B) Bearish debit spread
    (C) Bearish credit spread
    (D) Bullish credit spread

29. Paul writes 5 DEF Nov 35 calls at 3.50, and also writes 5 DEF Nov 35 puts at 3. What is Paul's maximum gain?

    (A) $3,250
    (B) Unlimited
    (C) $650
    (D) $3,000

30. An investor wrote KO put options. What other position would be grouped for calculating position limits?

    (A) Buying KO call options
    (B) Buying KO common stock
    (C) Buying KO put options
    (D) Selling KO call options

31. Which one of the following is a correct statement regarding adjustment of an options contract for an "odd stock split"? The number of shares per contract is:

    (A) increased
    (B) cancelled
    (C) unchanged
    (D) decreased

32. A speculator anticipates that the dollar will strengthen against the Swiss Franc. Which two of the following strategies could the speculator use to profit from his expectation?

    I.   Buy puts on the Swiss Franc
    II. Buy calls on the Swiss Franc
    III. Sell calls on the Swiss Franc
    IV. Sell puts on the Swiss Franc

    (A) I and II
    (B) I and III
    (C) II and III
    (D) II and IV

33. An investor received the following verbal confirmation from his broker: "You bought 1 KO Feb 30 call at 4 and sold 1 KO Feb 35 call at 1."What is the investor's maximum loss?

    (A) $300
    (B) $400
    (C) $100
    (D) Unlimited

34. Mr. Mero writes 1 uncovered HTZ May 40 put at 6. What is his maximum loss?

    (A) $3,400
    (B) $4,600
    (C) $4,000
    (D) $4,600

35. A customer purchases a T-bond July 100 call at 3.17. The customer will break even when the underlying T-bond trades:

    (A) $103,170
    (B) $1,031.70
    (C) $1,035.3125
    (D) $103,531.25

36. Which one of the following is a correct statement regarding adjustment of an options contract for an even stock split? The number of contracts is:

    (A) increased
    (B) decreased.
    (C) cancelled
    (D) unchanged

37. When is the latest possible time an option can be exercised by the holder? The:

    (A) third Friday of the expiration month at 5:30pm eastern time
    (B) Saturday following the third Friday at 11:59pm eastern time
    (C) third Friday of the expiration month at 11:59pm eastern time
    (D) Saturday following the third Friday at 5:30pm eastern time

38. An investor establishes the following position:

    Short 10 JPM Mar 45 calls at 8
    Long 10 JPM Mar 50 calls at 5

    In March, both options expire worthless. What is the resulting profit or loss?

    (A) $3,000 profit
    (B) $3,000 loss
    (C) $300 profit
    (D) $300 loss

39. A conservative investor owns a portfolio of well established companies that have a long history of high and uninterrupted dividends. She would like to increase the overall return on her portfolio. Which of the following strategies would be consistent with her goal?

    (A) Straddles
    (B) Covered Calls
    (C) Combinations
    (D) Puts

40. On October 5, 2010 an investor writes an ABC call option for 5. On February 8, 2011 the investor engages in a closing purchase for 3. What is the result for tax purposes?

    (A) $200 short-term capital gain
    (B) $200 long-term capital gain
    (C) $200 ordinary gain
    (D) $200 short-term capital loss

41. Marc buys 2 ABC May 70 calls at 4 and also buys 2 ABC May 70 puts at 3.50. What are Marc's break even points?

    I. $77.50
    II. $62.50
    III. $85
    IV. $55

    (A) I and II
    (B) I and III
    (C) II and III
    (D) II and IV

42. An investor sells 1 ABC July 35 call at 3. Which of the following statements best describes the investor's outlook and his potential maximum gain?

    (A) Bearish and has a potential maximum gain of $300
    (B) Bearish and has an unlimited potential maximum gain
    (C) Bullish and has a potential maximum gain of $300
    (D) Bullish and has an unlimited potential maximum gain

43. Which of the following combined positions is bullish?

    (A) Short put + long call
    (B) Short put + short call
    (C) Long put + long call
    (D) Long put + short call

44. A speculator believes the economy will be entering a recession. Using yield-based options, which two of the following positions would be consistent with his outlook?

    I.   Buy yield-based call options
    II. Write yield-based call options
    III. Buy yield-based put options
    IV. Write yield-based put options

    (A) I and III
    (B) I and IV
    (C) II and III
    (D) II and IV

45. Jake goes long an ABC Feb 40 call at 4 and goes short an ABC Feb 45 call at 3. What is Jake's maximum loss?

    (A) Unlimited
    (B) $400
    (C) $500
    (D) $100

46. An investor establishes the following position:

    Long 100 XOM stock at $75
    Short 1 XOM Aug 70 put at 3
    Short 1 XOM Aug 80 call at 4

    What is the customer's maximum gain?

    (A) $600
    (B) Unlimited gain
    (C) $900
    (D) $1,200

47. A customer sells an XYZ Feb 50 put at 3. Three weeks later, the put is exercised. What is the resulting tax consequence?

    (A) $5,000 sales proceeds
    (B) $4,700 sales proceeds
    (C) $4,700 cost basis
    (D) $5,000 cost basis

48. An investor sells short 1,000 XYZ at $50/share, and also writes 10 XYZ July 45 put at 3. What is the investor's margin requirement?

    (A) $28,000
    (B) $22,000
    (C) $23,500
    (D) $25,000

49. Tom has purchased 1 XYZ Feb 35 call at 3 and sold 1 XYZ 40 call at 2. What is Tom's breakeven point?

    (A) 45
    (B) 42
    (C) 38
    (D) 36

50. A portfolio manager of a multi-billion dollar portfolio believes that Standard & Poor's 500 Index is going to decline sharply over the next few months. Her portfolio is highly correlated to the S&P 500 Index. Which of the following is the most prudent course of action to protect against a decline in her portfolio?

    (A) Liquidate the entire portfolio
    (B) Purchase puts on each individual stock in the portfolio
    (C) Purchase puts on the S&P 500
    (D) Write calls on the S&P 500

OPTIONS EXPLANATIONS 7

1. **(B)**

Only covered calls may be written in a cash account. The writing of calls secured by cash equivalent to the aggregate strike is still considered naked or uncovered calls for margin purposes. Here is an example:

| Wrote 1 KLM Aug 50 call at 5 |
| Deposit of $5,000 cash |

Theoretically, KLM stock could rise to infinity. The investor would receive an assignment notice which would obligate him to sell KLM stock at $50/share. He would first need to go out to the market to purchase the stock at an infinite price. The $5,000 cash in the account would not offer him very much protection, so for margin purposes he would be naked or uncovered which only can be held in a margin account.

It is permissible to hold the following in a cash account:

- Writing cash secured puts (Choice A), upon assignment the investor would be obligated to purchase the stock at the strike price with cash held in the account;
- Debit Diagonal Call Spread (Choice C) since the most the investor could lose is the net debit paid;
- Debit Vertical Spreads (Choice D) since the most the investor could lose is the net debit paid

2. **(C)**

The customer has created a Covered Put Writing strategy, which in this context does not imply safety. "Covered" means covered for margin purposes whereby there is no additional margin requirement on the sale of the 5 XOM Sept 80 puts that the investor has written for a premium of 3. Therefore, the margin requirement would be limited to 50% of the short sale. Theoretically, the short sale of 500 shares of XOM has unlimited risk. The sale of 5 XOM puts does not offer the investor protection should XOM stock rise sharply.

3. **(D)**

When a customer exercises a put, the sales proceeds are determined as follows:

Exercise Price	- Premium	= Sales Proceeds
35	- 7	= 28
$3,500	- $700	= $2,800

Now since this is a Roman Numeral Format, the choices can be narrowed down to B or D. While, the question does not explicitly state that the stock was purchased in the market, we need to make an assumption that the customer purchased BKR in the market at $32/share or $3,200, exercised the put and sold the stock at $2,800. This resulted in a $400 loss.

4. **(A)**

The straddle writer is short both a call and a put on the same security, same expiration dates, and same strike prices. Writing the QRS Feb 65 call and put would establish a short straddle. Note premiums are not given in this question nor would the same premium be a requirement for a straddle.

5. **(B)**

The June 90 put would have the highest premium as it gives the holder the right to sell LTN at the highest possible price. All other features of a put being equal, the put with the highest strike price would have the highest premium.

6. **(A)**

The question asks for the "Best" reason for purchasing call options instead of the underlying stock. Options involve the use of leverage, which allows the investor to maximize his potential percentage return with the lowest cash outlay, and magnifying both risk and reward.

While the purchase of options instead of the underlying stock may involve lower transaction costs and/or a smaller cash commitment that would not be the "Best Reason" for purchasing options. Less risk would not be a reason for purchasing options instead of the underlying stock. The purchase of options instead of the underlying stock generally would involve greater risk.

7. **(C)**

A put buyers risk is limited to the premium or debit paid. Puts (and calls) allow for the use of leverage; with a smaller cash outlay as opposed to the short sale (or purchase) of the underlying security both risk and return are magnified. Put buyers may also use puts to hedge or protect against a decline in a long position as is the case with a Protective Put Purchase.

8. **(B)**

Before addressing the breakeven points of a Straddle it is important to note that T-Notes (and T-Bonds) are quoted as a percentage of par value + 1/32. So, a premium of 5.13 is 5% of par + 13/32.

A Straddle always has two breakeven points and is calculated as follows:

Strike price of call	+ Total premium	= Breakeven point
98.00	+ 5.13	= 103.13

Strike price of put	-Total premium	= Breakeven point
98.00	-5.13	=92.19

Let's further examine how we arrived at the breakeven point of 92.19:

98.00
- 5.13

While we can subtract 5 from 98, we cannot subtract 13/32 from 00/32, as we need the numerator to be larger than the denominator. So, we first need to borrow 1 (or 32/32) from the 98. It is then rewritten as follows:

97.32
- 5.13
92.19

9. **(C)**

Upon writing the SID option, Gary received a premium or credit of $600. Upon expiration, Gary realized a capital gain. After writing the option, only one of three possible outcomes will transpire:

- Gary may engage in a closing purchase
- Gary receives an assignment notice
- The option expires worthless

Since the option expired in 2011 and not 2010, Gary has a capital gain in the 2011. Note the goal of every option writer (both calls and puts) is to receive the premium with hopes that the option expires worthless, realizing a short-term capital gain.

10. **(B)**

Being short means that the customer is the seller of an option. To liquidate his existing position, he would need to engage in a closing transaction. Since he initially sold an option, he would now need to purchase an option. This would require a closing purchase.

It is important to remember that liquidating is synonymous with closing. However, liquidating may require the sale or purchase. So, liquidating an existing position would be either a closing sale or a closing purchase. Here is a summary of the two possibilities:

Initial Position…	Liquidating Position…
Opening Purchase	Closing Sale
Opening Sale	Closing Purchase

11. **(B)**

We approach this question by calculating the breakeven first. Since Trader Mike is bearish, he would earn a profit if the underlying stock traded below the breakeven point. Mike's breakeven point is calculated as follows:

Strike Price of Put	- Premium	= Breakeven Point
65	-3	= 62

Since Mike's breakeven point is $62, Mike will break even when ONM stock follows declines below$62, hence $61.25.

12. **(C)**

The customer created a Bull Spread. We will begin by rewriting the position as follows:

Transactions
Long 1 Swiss Franc Dec 55 Put
Sold 1 SF Dec 57 put (dominant leg)

Even though premiums are not given in the question, the put option with the higher strike would have a larger premium. We can now focus our attention on the put option with the higher strike price or premium. Since the investor is the seller of an SF Dec 57 put, he is bullish.
It is also a spread position in that it consists of the purchase and sale of either calls and puts on the same underlying security.

13. **(B)**

As a result of the two transactions, Carol realized an $8,000 loss. We can determine Carol's loss as follows:

Transaction	Debit or Credit
Sold short 1,000 ABC at $50	+$50,000 credit
Long 10 ABC Dec 55 calls at 3	-$3,000 debit
Exercise of call options	-$55,000 debit
Result = -$8,000 loss	

14. **(B)**

Pat has established a Net Debit Spread as follows:

Transaction	Debit or Credit
Bought 5 ABC June 50 calls	-5 debit
Sold 5 ABC June 55 calls	+2 credit
Net Debit = -3	

As an investor that has established a Net Debit Spread, he will profit if the spread widens. You can think of Pat as a Net Buyer since he established a Net Debit Spread. As a Net Buyer, Pat would like the spread to widen, meaning go from a lower price to a higher price. So, if Pat can sell the spread for more than the 3-point Net Debit that he paid, he will earn a profit, and that is what is meant by the term "widen".

15. **(B)**

The investor received a premium of 6.25 which is calculated as follows:

Premium (move decimal TWO places to the left)	X Contract Size	X Number of Contracts	= $ Aggregate Cost
.0625	X 10,000	X 1	$625

Note we first must move the decimal point on the premium TWO places to the left. Additionally, the contract size of the Canadian Dollar is 10,000. On all foreign currencies tested on the Series 7 exam with the exception of the Japanese Yen, we move the decimal point on the premium TWO places to the left, and the contract sizes are 10,000. Note it is irrelevant to the question that the Canadian Dollar is trading at 153.25.

16. **(B)**

Danny has created a Bullish Vertical Net Debit Spread which is rewritten as follows:

Transaction	Debit or Credit
Bought 1 DEF Apr 60 call	-$700 debit
Sold 1 DEF Apr 70 call	+$400 credit
Net Debit = -$300	

As the holder of a Net Debit Spread, Danny's maximum gain is limited to the difference between the two strike prices less the Net Debit. Let's now take a closer look at the difference between the two strike prices by exercising both options:

Transaction	Debit or Credit
Exercise of 1 DEF Apr 60 call	-$6,000 debit
Assignment of 1 DEF Apr 70 call	+$7,000 credit
Profit = -$1,000	

So, if DEF stock rose, Danny could exercise the Apr 60 call. However, if the stock rose above $70/share, the Apr 70 would be exercised and Danny would receive an assignment notice which would obligate him to sell the stock at $70. As a result, Danny's profit would be limited to $1,000 minus the net debit of $300 or a $700 profit.

17. **(A)**

Writing naked or uncovered calls has unlimited risk potential. Theoretically, the underlying stock could rise to infinity and the call option would be exercised by the buyer. This means that the naked call writer would receive an assignment notice which would trigger the obligation to sell the stock at the strike price. Since the naked call writer does not own the underlying stock, he would first need to purchase the stock in the market at an infinite price and then sell the stock at the strike price. Naked or uncovered call writing is only suitable for investors that understand and are willing to assume unlimited risk.

18. **(B)**
Pam has created a Horizontal Spread which consists of the purchase and sale of either calls or puts on the same security, same strike prices, but different expiration dates. Horizontal spreads are also known as Calendar Spreads or Time Spreads since there is a difference in expiration dates.

19. **(C)**

Dave has created a Combination which consists of the purchase or sale of a call(s) and put(s) on the same security with either different expiration dates and/or strike prices.

20. **(D)**

The investor has created a Covered Put Writing strategy. The Regulation T margin requirement is limited to 50% of the short sale or $25,000. There is no additional margin requirement on the sale of the put options. However, the question asked for the cash deposit, which is $22,000. The cash deposit is the margin requirement of $25,000 less the premium of $3,000 received. So the Federal Reserve (Regulation T) requires the investor to have $25,000 in the account. The investor would satisfy this requirement by depositing $22,000 cash since he would have a balance of $3,000 in the account already for the premium income received for writing the puts.

21. **(A)**

Sally is a straddle buyer, which means she is long both a call and a put on the same security, expiration dates, and strike prices. The maximum loss for the straddle buyer is limited to the total premium, which is the premium paid for the call ($500) plus the premium paid for the put ($450). The maximum loss would be realized if the underlying stock closes at $30/share at expiration. At $30/share, both the call and the put would expire worthless.

22. **(A)**

The straddle writer is short both a call and a put on the same security, expiration dates and strike prices. Writing the ABC June 80 call and ABC June 80 put would establish a short straddle. Note premiums are not given in this question nor would the same premium be a requirement for a straddle. Additionally, a straddle writer assumes unlimited risk because a naked call option is embedded in the straddle writer's position. Writing straddles is only suitable for investors that understand and are willing to assume such risk.

The other three choices are incorrect for the following reasons:

- Choice B - securities are different
- Choice C - the strike prices are different
- Choice D - the expiration dates are different

23. **(C)**

All Put Spreads (and Call Spreads) have limited risk.

Let us use an example to illustrate why a Debit Vertical Put Spread is bearish and subject to limited risk. An investor establishes a Bearish Vertical Debit Put Spread with the following position:

Transaction	Debit or Credit
Bought 1 XO Sept 30 Put = 3	-$300 debit
Sold 1 XO Sept 25 Put = 2	+200 credit
Net Debit = -$100	

By purchasing an XO Sept 30 Put at 3 and selling an XO Sept 25 Put at 2, the investor has a net debit of $100 or 1 point. The position has limited risk since the maximum loss is limited to the Net Debit of $100. The position is also bearish as the dominant leg of the spread is the option with the higher premium. Since the dominant leg is the purchase of a put, we are able to determine that the investor is bearish.

24. **(B)**

When the writer (seller) of an option receives an assignment notice, this means that the buyer has made the decision to exercise his option. The writer now has an obligation to buy or sell the underlying security.

25. **(A)**

The position is a Protective Put Purchase which consists of a long stock position and a long put(s). Ron is long 3 DEF puts only as an insurance policy to protect against a decline in his long DEF stock position.

The breakeven point for a Protective Put Purchase can be expressed as follows:

Purchase Price of Stock	+ Premium	= Breakeven Point
$40/share	+ 5	= $45/share

So, Ron needs DEF stock to rise to $45/share to recoup the 5-point premium paid for the puts. So, at $45/share, the following would result: Ron's DEF stock, which was purchased at $40/share, is sold at $45/share resulting in a 5-point profit. The 5-point profit on the sale of the stock is offset against the 5-point premium paid for the put options. The result is no gain or loss.

26. **(B)**

A put writer who is short the underlying stock has unlimited risk (I). Theoretically, a short seller has unlimited risk as a stock could rise to infinity. In the event of a rise in the stock, being the writer or seller of a put would not add any protection. The put writer would have the obligation (but, not the right) to buy the underlying stock at the exercise price or strike price. In the event of a rise in the stock, the put would be out of the money, and the put writer would not receive an exercise notice, therefore having no control over covering his short stock position.

(IV) Describes a straddle writer which has unlimited risk, as a naked call option is embedded in the position.

27. **(A)**

Choice A is a Protective Call Purchase and has limited risk. However, since the position includes a short sale of stock, it can only be executed in a margin account. It is permissible to hold the following positions in a cash account:

- Long Put (Choice B) as the most the investor could lose is the premium or debit paid;
- Long Straddle (Choice C) as the most the investor could lose is the total premium or total debit paid;
- Covered call Writing (D) as the most the investor could lose is stock position minus the premium received or credit for writing the call option

28. **(B)**

Let us take a closer examination of the position:

Transaction	Bullish or Bearish	Debit or Credit
Bought 1 XYZ May 55 Put = 5	Bearish	-$500 debit
Sold 1 XYZ May 50 Put = 3	Bullish	+300 credit
Net Debit = -$200		

By purchasing an XYZ May 55 Put at 5 and selling an XYZ May 50 Put at 3, the investor has a net debit of $200. The position is also bearish as the dominant leg of the spread is the option with the higher premium. Since the dominant leg is the purchase of a put, we are able to determine that the investor is bearish.

29. **(A)**

You should be able to identify Paul's position as a short straddle (straddle writer). The straddle writer is short both a call(s) and a put(s) on the same security, expiration dates, strike prices. The maximum gain for Paul (or any straddle writer) would be the total premium received for writing the straddle. The total premium is 6.50. Here is how to determine the premium in dollars:

Total premium	X number of contracts	x contract size	= $Premium
6.50	X 5	= 100	=$3,250

Ideally, at expiration, Paul would like the stock to close exactly at $35/share at expiration. At $35/share, both options are at-the-money and would expire worthless. Paul would then keep the total premium received without receiving an assignment notice from either the put or the call buyer.

30. **(A)**

For purposes of calculating position limits, we must first categorized positions as being on the same side of the market. Positions on the same side of the market are bullish versus bearish option positions which are grouped as follows:

Bullish Side of Market	Bearish Side of Market
Buying KO call options	Buying KO put options
Writing KO put option	Writing KO call options

31. **(A)**

Option contracts are affected by an odd stock split in that the exercise price decreases while the number of shares per contract increases proportionally. Note, the number of contracts remain unchanged.

Let us review an example: Tom owns 1 ABC May 90 call. The company announces a 3 for 2 stock split, which means Tom will receive 3 shares for every 2 shares that he owns. Following the split, Tom will now own 1 ABC June 60 call. Note, the number of shares per contract is now 150 (3/2 x 100 shares per original contract), 30 exercise price (2/3 x 90 exercise price). Also note the aggregate exercise price remains unchanged at $9,000.

32. **(B)**

The speculator anticipates that the dollar will strengthen against the Swiss Franc. Stated another way, the speculator believes the Swiss Franc will weaken or decline in value. As a result, the speculator should assume bearish positions on the Swiss Franc which are: buying puts and selling calls.

33. **(A)**

The investor established a Bullish Vertical Debit Call Spread. The investor's maximum loss is limited to his Net Debit as follows:

Transaction	Debit or Credit
Bought 1 KO Feb 30 call at 4	-$400 debit
Sold 1 KO Feb 35 call at 1	+$100 credit
Net Debit = -$300	

The maximum loss to the investor is the Net Debit or total premium of $300 for establishing the spread.

34. (A)

The uncovered put writer realizes his maximum loss upon assignment. Mr. Mero would be obligated to purchase the stock at the strike price. His maximum loss can be expressed as follows:

Aggregate Exercise Price	- Premium	= Maximum Loss
-$4,000	-$600	=-$3,400

If Mr. Mero receives an assignment notice, he would be obligated to purchase 100 shares of HTZ stock at the exercise price of $40 for a total cost of $4,000. Theoretically, HTZ stock could decline to zero, resulting in a $4,000 loss on the stock less the $600 premium received.

35. (D)

Here is the formula for determining the breakeven:

Strike Price of call	+ Premium	= Breakeven
100	+ 3.17	= 103.17

It is important to remember that T-bond options are quoted as a percentage of par + 1/32. Par value is equal to $1,000. The value of 1/32 = $31.25 ($1,000/32 = $31.25).

Percentage of Par	+ 1/32
103% X $100,000	+ (17 x $31.25)
$103,000	+ $531.25
= $103,531.25	

36. (A)

Option contracts are effected by even split in that the exercise price decreases while the number of contracts increases proportionally.

Let us review an example: Jack owns 1 ABC June 50 call. The company announces a 2 for 1 stock split, which means Jack will receive 2 shares for every 1 share he owns. Following the split, Jack will now own 2 ABC June 25 calls. Note the number of contracts increases while the exercise price or strike price decreases proportionally. Two contracts (2/1 x 1 original contract), 25 exercise price (1/2 x 50 exercise price). Also note the aggregate exercise price remains unchanged at $5,000.

37. (A)

The very latest time that an option can be exercised is the third Friday of the expiration month at 5:30pm eastern time. This should not be confused with the options expiration date. Options expire on the Saturday following the third Friday at 11:59pm eastern time.

38. (A)

The investor earns a $3,000 profit calculated as follows:

Transaction	Debit or Credit
Short 10 JPM Mar 45 calls at 8	+$8,000 credit
Long 10 JPM Mar 50 calls at 5	-$5,000 debit
+$3,000 Credit	

The investor is a net creditor or net seller which is his maximum gain.

39. **(B)**

Covered call writing is suitable for an investor with a conservative risk profile. This is also an income-generating strategy as the calls are written to generate income. This strategy is popular with dividend paying stocks. So, the investor receives dividend income from the underlying stock in addition to the premium income received for writing the options.

40. **(A)**

The investor has created a $200 short-term capital gain. Here is the method for approaching this:

Sales Proceeds	- Cost Basis	= Capital Gain or Loss
$500	- $300	= $200

This a short-term capital gain because the holding period does not exceed a 12-month period. The holding period is always going to be short-term when the position is initiated by a sale of an option. The rationale is that a holding period has not been established because the position was not initiated with a purchase.

41. **(A)**

You should be able to identify the position as a Long Straddle. The straddle buyer is long both a call and a put on the same security, same expiration dates and same strike prices. The straddle buyer expects "volatility" in the underlying security. Stated another way, straddle buyers are neither bullish nor bearish, but expect the stock to fluctuate in a wide range. Let us now take a closer look at Marc's position:

Transaction	Debit
Bought 2 ABC May 70 calls	= 4
Bought 2 ABC May 70 puts	= 3.50
Total Debit = 7.50	

Marc has two breakeven points which can be expressed as follows:

Strike Price of Call	+ Total Debit	= Upside Breakeven Point
70	+ 7.50	= 77.50

Strike Price of Put	- Total Debit	= Downside Breakeven Point
70	- 7.50	= 62.50

So, Marc earns a profit if ABC stock trades above $77.50 (upside breakeven point) below $62.50 (downside breakeven point). This is consistent with the outlook of a straddle buyer in that he expects volatility.

42. **(A)**

The selling or writing of a call option is a bearish strategy, as the writer will benefit if the option expires worthless by the underlying stock closing at $35/share or lower at expiration. The writer's maximum potential gain is limited to the $300 premium or credit received for selling the option.

43. **(A)**

Short puts and long calls are bullish positions.

A put writer (short put) has an obligation (if assigned) to purchase the stock at the strike price, therefore establishing a long stock position (bullish).

A long call is also bullish, as it allows the holder to exercise the call, acquiring a long stock position.

44. **(C)**

Since the speculator believes the economy is going to enter a recession, the Federal Reserve Board would pursue an easy money policy or lower interest rates.

Yield-based options can be utilized to speculate on the direction of the yield or interest rate. With an expectation of declining interest rates, the speculator can best position himself by writing yield-based calls and buying yield-based puts.

45. **(D)**

This is a bullish vertical call debit spread which can be expressed as follows:

Transaction	Debit or Credit
Long 1 ABC Feb 40 call	= -4 (debit)
Short 1 ABC Feb 45 call 3	= +3 (credit)
Net Debit = 1	

Jake's maximum loss is limited to the net debit of 1 point or $100.

46. **(D)**

The three positions can be rearranged into two strategies as follows:

Covered Call Writing
Long 100 XOM stock at $75
Short 1 XOM Aug 80 Call at 4
Maximum gain = $900

The Covered Call Writing strategy has a maximum gain limited to $900.

Short Put
Short 1 XOM Aug 70 put at 3
Maximum gain = $300 credit

The short put has a maximum gain or credit limited to the premium received of $300. Overall, the customer's maximum gain is limited to $1,200; $900 for the covered call, and $300 for the short put.

47. **(C)**

The customer initially receives a premium of $300 for writing the put option. When the put is exercised, the customer receives an assignment notice which obligates him to purchase 100 shares of XYZ at the strike price of 50 or $5,000. We can determine the customer's cost basis as follows:

Aggregate Exercise Price	-	Premium	= Cost Basis
$5,000	-	$300	= $4,700

48. **(D)**

The customer has created a Covered Put Writing strategy. Covered in this context does not imply safety. Covered means "covered for margin purposes" whereby there is no additional margin requirement deposit on the sale of the 10 XYZ July 45 puts that the investor has written for a premium of 3. Therefore, the margin requirement is limited to 50% of the short sale proceeds.

49. **(D)**

Tom has created a Bullish Vertical Spread. We will begin by rewriting the position as follows:

Transactions	Premium
Bought 1 XYZ Feb 35 Call	= -3 (debit)
Sold 1 XYZ Feb 40 Call	= +2 (credit)
Net debit = -1	

We can now apply the following formula to determine the breakeven point:

Strike Price of the dominant leg of the spread (leg with the higher premium)	+ Net Debit (note that we add the net amount for call spreads; if this was a put spread we would subtract the net amount)	= Breakeven Point
35	+ 1	= 36

So, Tom breaks even when XYZ stock trades $36/share. At $36/share, Tom could exercise his XYZ Feb 35 call, buying the stock at $35/share and then selling the stock in the market at $36/share. Tom would earn a 1-point profit, recouping his 1-point net debit paid for the spread.

50. **(C)**

The most prudent course of action is the purchase of puts on the S&P 500 Index. A long put would be the best method of protecting or hedging a long position. A long put is used only as an insurance policy to protect against a decline in the long position. Under the worst possible outcome, the portfolio manager would profit on the put from the strike price all the way down to zero. To a large degree, this would offset the losses incurred on the stock portfolio, essentially providing an effective hedge.

OPTIONS EXAM 8

1. Hale writes 1 ABC July 45 straddle at 7. At what price will the underlying stock need to trade at expiration for Hale to realize the maximum gain?

   (A) $45
   (B) $50
   (C) $40
   (D) $46

2. An RR would like to place an options advertisement in the Main Street Journal. Which one of the following statements is correct? This advertisement must:

   (A) be pre-approved by a ROP
   (B) include the RR's performance of all past recommendations
   (C) be filed with CBOE
   (D) be filed with the OCC

3. Which two of the following are examples of narrow-based index options?

   I.   CBOE Gold Index Options
   II. S&P 500 Index Options
   III. CBOE Internet Index Options
   IV. Amex Major Market Index Options

   (A) I and II
   (B) I and III
   (C) II and III
   (D) II and IV

4. Which one of the following is a correct statement regarding the adjustment of an options contract for a stock dividend? The number of contracts is:

   (A) decreased.
   (B) increased
   (C) unchanged
   (D) cancelled

5. Which strategy has unlimited gain potential?

   (A) Short Swiss Franc put option
   (B) Long Euro call option
   (C) Short Yen call option
   (D) Long British Pound put

6. Mike has initialed the following strategy:

   Long 1 DO Apr 60 put
   Short 1 DO Apr 65 put

   Which two of the following outcomes would be favorable for Mike?

   I.   DO stock decreases in value
   II. DO stock increases in value
   III. Both options are exercised
   IV. Both options expire without being exercised

   (A) I and III
   (B) I and IV
   (C) II and III
   (D) II and IV

7. An investor buys 5 XDA (Australian Dollar) Mar 95 calls at 2.03. What is the investor required to deposit?

   (A) $1,015
   (B) $203
   (C) $2,030
   (D) $10,150

8. An investor engaged in a closing purchase. His initial transaction was:

   (A) a closing sale.
   (B) a closing purchase.
   (C) an opening sale.
   (D) an opening purchase.

9. An investor is long a DEF Feb 65 put. The addition of which of the following positions would create a bull spread?

    (A) Short DEF Feb 60 put
    (B) Short DEF Feb 70 put
    (C) Short DEF Feb 70 call
    (D) Long DEF Feb 65 call

10. Larry goes long 3 JNJ Oct 65 calls at a premium of 5. With JNJ stock trading at $67, how much time value do the call options have?

    (A) 2 points
    (B) 3 points
    (C) 5 points
    (D) 0 points

11. Which two of the following would establish a vertical debit spread?

    I.   Long 1 NMO Nov 55 put
    II. Short 1 MNO Dec 60 put
    III. Long 1 MNO Dec 65 put
    IV. Short 1 MNO Nov 60 put

    (A) I and III
    (B) I and IV
    (C) II and III
    (D) II and IV

12. Best Buy (U.S. company) will be importing flat screen televisions from Panasonic (Japanese Company). Best Buy has agreed to make payments in Japanese Yen to Panasonic. How should Best Buy hedge its position?

    (A) Buy calls on the Japanese Yen
    (B) Buy puts on the Japanese Yen
    (C) Write calls on the Japanese Yen
    (D) Write puts on the Japanese Yen

13. Which option strategy carries the greatest potential for reward?

    (A) Writing uncovered puts
    (B) Writing uncovered calls
    (C) Buying puts
    (D) Buying calls

14. Sandy is short 3 EBAY Jan 30 puts at 3 and also short 3 Jan 30 calls at 3.50. What is her maximum potential loss?

    (A) $650
    (B) $975
    (C) $1,950
    (D) Unlimited

15. All of the following strategies have unlimited risk Except:

    (A) Short call
    (B) Short put
    (C) Short Straddle
    (D) Short Combination

16. A customer goes long an Australian Dollar Oct 50 call and short an Australian Dollar Oct 52 call. This customer has established a:

    (A) Bull spread
    (B) Bear spread
    (C) Combination
    (D) Hedge

17. Marc is the holder of 1 ABC July 60 call. Shortly after the purchase, ABC stock splits 2 for 1. After the split, which of the following correctly reflects Marc's position?

    (A) 2 ABC July 30 calls; 100 shares per contract
    (B) 1 ABC July 30 calls; 150 shares per contract
    (C) 2 ABC July 60 call; 100 shares per contract
    (D) 1 ABC July 120 call; 100 shares per contract

18. George buys 500 shares of PFE at 40 and also buys 5 PFE Aug 40 puts at 5. Which one of the following statements is correct? George:

(A) is neutral on PFE stock.
(B) is bearish on PFE stock.
(C) would like his put options to expire worthless.
(D) would like his put options to go deep in-the-money.

19. Sue writes an Oct 25 call at 6. Which two of the following best describe this strategy?

I. Bullish strategy
II. Bearish strategy
III. Limited loss potential
IV. Unlimited loss potential

(A) I and III
(B) I and IV
(C) II and III
(D) II and IV

20. Bob is the writer of 3 XYZ Aug 50 calls. Shortly after the sale, XYZ stock splits 3 for 2. Following the split, which of the following correctly reflects Bob's position?

(A) 3 XYZ Aug 33.33 calls
(B) 3 XYZ Aug 50 calls
(C) 4.5 XYZ Aug 33.33 calls
(D) 3 XYZ Aug 50 calls

21. An investor created the following position:

Long 1 VZ Dec 35 put
Short 1 VZ Dec 40 put

Which two characteristics are TRUE of this position?

I. Debit
II. Credit
III. Bullish
IV. Bearish

(A) I and III
(B) I and IV
(C) II and III
(D) II and IV

22. Theresa writes 10 XYZ Mar 50 calls at 3. These calls will be in-the-money when the underlying stock is trading at:

(A) $46
(B) $50
(C) $52
(D) $49

23. Morty goes long 10 ABC Jan 50 puts for a premium of 7. ABC stock then declines to $38/share. Morty purchases 1,000 shares of ABC at the market and immediately exercises the puts. According to tax rules, the sales proceeds received by Morty are:

(A) $38,000
(B) $57.000
(C) $43,000
(D) $50,000

24. An investor writes 3 XDN (Japanese Yen) Oct 120 puts for 4.17 and later engages in a closing purchase for 3.11. What is the resulting profit or loss?

(A) $318 profit
(B) $318 loss
(C) $106 profit
(D) $106 loss

25. An investor goes long 5 DEF June 25 calls at 3 and also goes long 5 DEF June 20 puts at 2. What are the investor's break even points?

I. $28
II. $18
III. $30
IV. $15

(A) I and II
(B) I and III
(C) II and III
(D) III and IV

26. An investor purchases 2 ABC May 65 puts at 3. What is the Regulation T requirement?

(A) 100%
(B) 50%
(C) 0%
(D) 25%

27. Stacy writes 1 XYZ June 35 call at 2 and also writes 1 XYZ June 35 puts at 1. At what two of the following prices does Stacy break even?

    I. $38
    II. $32
    III. $37
    IV. $34

    (A) I and II
    (B) I and III
    (C) II and III
    (D) II and IV

28. An investor buys an ABC Mar 55 put for 5 and also writes an ABC Mar 50 put for 3. What is the investor's breakeven point per share?

    (A) $53
    (B) $50
    (C) $47
    (D) $48

29. Adam buys 1 ABC Oct 65 call and sells 1 ABC Oct 70 call. Which two of the following are characteristics of this strategy?

    I.   Credit
    II. Debit
    III. Bullish
    IV. Bearish

    (A) I and III
    (B) I and IV
    (C) II and III
    (D) II and IV

30. A customer places an initial trade to sell 3 XYZ Sept 60 calls at 3. The branch office which maintains the customer's account does not receive an executed customer agreement within the allotted time. Which of the following orders may the RR accept from the customer?

    (A) Buy 3 XYZ Sept 60 calls
    (B) Buy 3 ABC Sept 60 calls
    (C) Buy 3 XYZ Oct 60 calls
    (D) Buy 3 XYZ Sept 50 calls

31. Joe buys 1 ABC Sept 65 put and sells 1 ABC Sept 70 put. This is an example of a:

    (A) Strangle
    (B) Straddle
    (C) Combination
    (D) Spread

32. Mr. Williams establishes the following position in his options account:

    Short 100 shares of DEF at $50
    Short 1 DEF Feb 45 put at 2

    What is Mr. Williams's maximum gain?

    (A) Unlimited
    (B) $700
    (C) $300
    (D) $500

33. On Apr 16, 2010 Bruce is contemplating the purchase of put options on PWE stock. Which one of the following options would have the smallest premium?

    (A) June 75 puts
    (B) June 70 puts
    (C) June 90 puts
    (D) June 85 puts

34. Zack went long 2 Apr 140 British Pound calls at 3. What is Zack's maximum loss?

    (A) $300
    (B) $600
    (C) $3,000
    (D) $6,000

35. Hale writes 3 Swiss Franc Apr 110 calls at 5. How can this strategy be characterized?

    I.   Bearish
    II. Bullish
    III. Limited loss potential
    IV. Unlimited loss potential

    (A) I and III
    (B) I and IV
    (C) II and III
    (D) II and IV

36. Robert buys 1 ABC Oct 65 call and sells 1 ABC June 70 call. Which two of the following are characteristics of this strategy?

   I.   Credit
   II. Debit
   III. Bullish
   IV. Bearish

   (A) I and III
   (B) I and IV
   (C) II and III
   (D) II and IV

37. An investor is bearish on APPL stock. She is in the process of deciding whether she should sell APPL stock short or purchase put options on APPL. All of the following are advantages of purchasing puts as opposed selling the stock short EXCEPT:

   (A) greater leverage
   (B) limited loss potential
   (C) exempt from Regulation SHO
   (D) finite life

38. A customer buys 5 three-year LEAPS on IBM for a premium of 14. What is the customer's total purchase price?

   (A) $7,000
   (B) $210
   (C) $21,000
   (D) $1,400

39. A customer of Auto-Ex Brokerage sells short 500 shares of XOM at $75 and also writes 5 XOM Sept 80 puts at 3. What is the investor's required cash deposit?

   (A) $17,250
   (B) $18,750
   (C) $36,000
   (D) $37,500

40. Hale buys 100 shares of AT&T stock at $30. He also goes long 1 AT&T Sept 25 put at 3. At what price does AT&T stock need to trade for Hale to earn a profit?

   (A) $33/share
   (B) $34/share
   (C) $21/share
   (D) $22/share

41. Alice just bought an XYZ May 35 call at 6. In which of the following scenarios would Alice lose her entire premium? At expiration, XYZ stock is trading:

   I.   Below its strike price
   II. Above its strike price
   III. At its strike price

   (A) I only
   (B) II only
   (C) I and III only
   (D) II and III only

42. Broad-based index options cease trading each day at:

   (A) 4:15pm eastern time
   (B) 11:59pm eastern time
   (C) 5:30pm eastern time
   (D) 4:00pm eastern time

43. An investor exercises an IBM June 50 call at 3. In his cash account, what is the required deposit?

   (A) $2,500
   (B) $2,200
   (C) $5,000
   (D) $4,700

44. An investor writes an SPX (S&P 500) June 1240 index put. At expiration, the index settled at 1225. The writer must:

   (A) take physical delivery of the index at 1240
   (B) make physical delivery of the index at 1240
   (C) deliver $1,500 cash to the buyer
   (D) purchase the index for $124,000

45. Zack writes 1 LMN Apr 30 put at 3. Which two of the following best describe this strategy?

   I.   Bearish
   II. Bullish
   III. Unlimited Risk
   IV. Limited Risk

   (A) I and III
   (B) I and IV
   (C) II and III
   (D) II and IV

46. A debit call spread can be created from which two of the following?

   I.   Long 1 ABC Oct 80 call
   II. Short 1 ABC Oct 80 call
   III. Long 1 ABC Oct 85 call
   IV. Short 1 ABC Oct 85 call

   (A) I and IIII
   (B) I and IV
   (C) II and III
   (D) II and IV

47. An investor buys a KO June 65 call at 4 and a KO June 65 put at 3.75. What is this called?

   (A) Long combination
   (B) Diagonal spread
   (C) Long Strangle
   (D) Long straddle

48. Which one of the following strategies has the greatest loss potential?

   (A) Selling uncovered calls
   (B) Selling covered puts
   (C) Selling covered calls
   (D) Selling uncovered puts

49. Jack purchased 500 shares of ABC at $45 and also bought 5 ABC Mar 40 puts at 3. Six months later, ABC is trading at $45 and the puts expire worthless. What is Jack's resulting loss?

   (A) $1,500 loss
   (B) $300 loss
   (C) $500 loss
   (D) $0

50. An investor writes 2 ABC June 40 puts at 7. At what price would the underlying stock need to trade for the investor to break even?

   (A) $54
   (B) $26
   (C) $47
   (D) $33

OPTIONS EXPLANATIONS 8

1. **(A)**

As a writer of a straddle, Hale expects ABC stock to trade within a narrow range. At expiration, Hale will achieve his maximum gain if both the put and the call expire worthless. At $45/share, both the call and the put would expire worthless as both options would be at-the-money, having zero intrinsic value. Hale's maximum gain would be the premium received of 7 points or $700.

2. **(A)**

An advertisement is any form of communication in which the broker-dealer cannot control the audience that is viewing, reading, or listening to the communication. Examples include: newspaper advertisements, websites, and radio & television commercials. Option advertisements are of particular concern to FINRA in that they are a complex product, and the broker-dealer cannot control the audience that is viewing the communication. As a result, options advertisements must be approved by a Registered Options Principal (ROP), and filed with FINRA ten days prior to first use

3. **(B)**

The CBOE Gold Index Options and the CBOE Internet Index Options are examples of narrow-based index options. This is because the index is limited to one industry or sector of the market. These index options tend to have more volatility as they are not diversified across industry lines as are broad-based index options. The S&P 500 Index Options and the Amex major Market Index Options are diversified across industry lines and are therefore broad-based index options.

4. **(C)**

A stock dividend is treated in the same manner as an odd stock split. That is, the number of shares per contract increases while the exercise price or strike price decreases proportionally. For example, Scott owns 1 DEF Nov 50 call. The company declares a 10% stock dividend. Scott still owns 1 contract, but it is now based on 110 shares. (100 shares x 10% = 10 additional shares)

5. **(B)**

Long call options have unlimited gain potential, as theoretically the underlying currency (or security) could rise to infinity. Both short puts and short calls have a maximum gain limited to the premium or credit received. Long puts also have limited gain potential as the underlying currency (or security) can only decline to zero.

6. **(D)**

Mike has created a Bullish Vertical Credit Put Spread. We will begin by rewriting the position as follows:

Transactions
Long 1 DO Apr 60 put
Short 1 DO Apr 65 put (dominant position)

Even though premiums are not given in the question, the put option with the higher strike would have a larger premium. We can now focus our attention on the put option with the higher strike price or premium. Since Mike has sold the DO Apr 65 put, he would have a net credit or be a net seller. Since Mike is a net seller, he would want both options to expire without being exercised (Choice IV). In addition, the sale of the Apr 65 put would also be bullish (Choice II).

7. **(A)**

When purchasing an option, the Regulation T margin requirement is 100% of the premium. Now we must determine what the premium translates into dollars. The investor paid a premium of 2.03 which is calculated as follows:

Premium (move decimal TWO places to the left)	X Contract Size	X Number of Contracts	= $ Aggregate Cost
.0203	X 10,000	X 5	$1,015

Note we first must move the decimal point on the premium TWO places to the left. Additionally, the contract size of the Australian Dollar is 10,000. On all foreign currencies tested on the Series 7 exam with the exception of the Japanese Yen, we move the decimal point on the premium TWO places to the left, and the contract size is 10,000.

8. **(C)**

Since the investor engaged in a closing purchase, his initial transaction was an opening sale. Here is an example:

Opening Sale	Sold 1 ABC Mar 90 Call
Closing Purchase	Bought 1 ABC Mar 90 Call

Here is another example whereby the initial transaction is a purchase:

Opening Purchase	Bought 1 ABC Mar 90 Call
Closing Sale	Sold 1 ABC Mar 90 Call

9. **(B)**

Since the investor is long a DEF Feb 65 put, he would need to go short (write) a put with a higher strike price to establish a bull spread. Let us now take a closer look at the position:

Transactions
long a DEF Feb 65 put
Short DEF Feb 70 put *(dominant leg)*

Even though premiums are not given in the question, the put option with the higher strike would have a larger premium. We can now focus our attention on the put option with the higher strike price or premium. Since the investor has sold the DEF Feb 70 put (dominant leg), he is bullish.

10. **(B)**

The Time Value of an option is determined as follows:

Option Premium	-	Intrinsic Value	= Time Value

So, first we need to determine if the option has any intrinsic value or money value. A call option is in-the-money if the exercise price is below the market price of the underlying stock. Since the exercise price is below the market price by 2 points, the option has 2 points of intrinsic value. The remaining 3 points is the option's time value.

Now let's go back to our example:

Option Premium	-	Intrinsic Value	= Time Value
5	-	2	= 3

The key is to first determine whether or not an option has intrinsic value before attempting to determine the options time value. Whatever amount remains is the time value.

11. **(C)**

A Vertical Debit Spread can be established with puts by purchasing (long) the put with the higher strike price (given that they have the same expiration dates) and writing or selling (short) the put with the lower strike price. The put with the higher strike price would have a higher premium than the put option sold, resulting in a net debit. Vertical spreads have different strike prices, but the same expiration dates.

12. **(A)**

As a U.S. company, Best Buy is concerned about currency risk. As an importer, Best Buy has agreed to make payment to Panasonic in Japanese Yen. Since Best Buy will be paying in Yen, the fear or risk is that the Yen will rise against the U.S. dollar. When it is time to exchange U.S. dollars for Yen, the U.S. dollars will purchase less Yen. Effectively, this will increase Best Buy's costs on flat screen televisions. To hedge against a rise in the Yen, the Best Buy should buy calls on the Yen. So if the Yen does rise against the dollar, any loss in the foreign exchange market would be offset against an increase in value in the Yen call options.

13. **(D)**

Buying call options has unlimited upside potential. The holder of the call could exercise the option, and purchase the underlying stock at the strike price. Theoretically, the stock could rise to infinity, giving the call buyer unlimited upside potential.

Writing uncovered calls and puts carries limited upside potential. The writer of an option (whether a call or put) has a maximum gain limited to the premium received. Buying puts has limited upside potential as a stock can only decline to zero. For example, an investor is long the ABC Sept 30 put at 3. If ABC stock declines to zero, the investor could buy the stock at zero and exercise his put (selling his stock at $30/share). His maximum gain would be limited to the exercise price minus the premium paid ($2,700).

14. **(D)**

Sandy has written a Straddle. The key concept is that embedded in the straddle writer's position is a naked or uncovered call option. The naked call option lends the position to unlimited risk. Theoretically, the underlying stock could rise to infinity. The call option would be exercised by the buyer. This means the straddle writer would receive an assignment notice which would trigger the obligation to sell the stock at the strike price. Since the straddle writer does not own the underlying stock, it would first need to be purchased in the market at an infinite price and then sold at the strike price.

Like the naked call writer, the straddle writer has unlimited risk, and is only suitable for investors that understand and are willing to assume such risk.

15. **(B)**

Note that this is an "Except" question. The correct answer is the strategy that has limited risk. The writer of a put (short put) has limited risk in that the maximum loss is limited to the exercise price – premium. Let us review an example:

Short 1 ABC June 50 put = 3

The maximum loss can be expressed as follows:

Aggregate Exercise Price	-	Premium	= Maximum Loss
$5,000	-	$300	= $4,700

In a worst case scenario, ABC stock declines to zero and the writer is obligated to purchase the stock at $50/share or $5,000. The investor will lose $5,000 on the stock less the premium of $300 which was received.

16. **(A)**

The customer has established a Bull Spread, which consists of the purchase (long) and sale (short) of either calls or puts on the same currency (or security). Depending on the type of spread, the expiration dates and/or strike prices may be the same or different. We will begin by rewriting the position to see how we determined that this is a bull spread:

Transactions
Long 1 Australian Dollar Oct 50 call *(dominant leg)*
Short 1 Australian Dollar Oct 52 call

Even though premiums are not provided in the question, the call option with the lower strike would have a larger premium (dominant leg). We can now focus our attention on the call option with the lower strike price. Since the customer has bought an Australian Oct 50 call, he is bullish.

17. **(A)**

The first step in the process is being able to identify an even stock split, which always ends in a ratio of 1. Examples include 2 for 1, 3 for 1, 4 for 1, and 5 for 1, etc. In the case of a 2 for 1 stock split each shareholder will receive two shares for each share that they own. Even splits also effect option contracts as follows:

- The number of contracts increases; and
- The strike price decreases proportionally

Following the split, Marc now owns 2 ABC July 30 calls which can be determined as follows:

Prior to Split...	Multiplier	After Split...
1 contract	2/1 or 2	2 contracts
Exercise price of 60	½ or 50%	Exercise price of 30

Note, the aggregate exercise price remains unchanged at $6,000.

18. **(C)**

The position is a Protective Put Purchase, which consists of a long stock position and a long put(s).

George has purchased put options as only an insurance policy to protect against a decline in his long PFE stock position. So, he would like his insurance policy (put options) to expire worthless. The best possible outcome for George would be an increase in PFE stock. In theory, PFE stock could increase to an infinite price, yielding George an unlimited gain on the stock. George would not exercise his put options, and as a result, would only lose the $2,500 premium paid for the puts.

Choices A and B are incorrect since a Protective Put Purchase is a bullish position. Choice D is incorrect since George would not like his put options to go deep in-the-money as that would mean that his stock position has substantially declined in value.

19. **(D)**

Writing a call option is a bearish strategy, as the writer would like the option to trade at or below the strike at expiration so the call option expires worthless. Since the question does not indicate that Sue owns the stock, she has written an uncovered or naked call option. As a result, Sue is subject to unlimited loss potential. Theoretically, the underlying stock could rise to infinity. The call option would be exercised by the buyer. This means that as the writer of a naked call, Sue would receive an assignment notice which would trigger the obligation to sell the stock at the strike price. Since Sue does not own the underlying stock, she would first need to go out to the market to purchase the stock in the market at an infinite price and then sell the stock to the buyer at the strike price.

20. **(A)**

The first step in the process is being able to identify an odd stock split. An odd stock split always ends with a ratio of other than 1. Examples include 3 for 2, 4 for 3, 5 for 2, etc. In the case of a 3 for 2 stock split each shareholder will receive three shares for every two shares that they own.

Odd splits also affect option contracts as follows:

- The number of shares per contact increases (the number of contracts remain the same); and
- The strike price decreases proportionally

Following the split, Bob now owns 3 XYZ Aug 50 calls which can be determined as follows:

Prior to Split...	Multiplier	After Split...
3 contract with a contract size of 100 shares per contact	3/2 or 1.5	3 contracts with a contract size of 150 shares per contract
Exercise price of 50	2/3 or 67%	Exercise price of 33.33

Note the aggregate exercise price remains unchanged at $15,000.

21. **(C)**

This is a Bullish Credit Spread. The first step is being able to identify that this is a credit spread. Even though no premiums are given, you can determine that the put option with the Higher Strike Price has a higher premium (since the expiration dates are the same).

The investor writes or sells the 40 put which brings in more money that is paid out for the 35 put. As a result, the investor is a "net seller" or has established a credit spread. Ideally a net seller or writer would like both options to expire worthless. To determine whether the investor is bullish or bearish, focus on the dominant leg of the spread. The dominant leg is the 40 put, since it would have a higher premium. Writing or selling a Dec 40 put is a bullish strategy.

22. **(C)**

Call options have intrinsic value or are in-the-money when the exercise price is below the market price of the underlying security. As a result, the XYZ Mar 50 calls are in-the-money when the XYZ stock is trading at $52/share. It is important to note that we only focus on the relationship between the exercise price and the underlying security. In other words, do not take into consideration whether the investor is the buyer or writer of the option.

23. **(C)**

The premium paid for purchasing the puts is subtracted from the exercise price of the puts as follows:

Strike Price (from exercise of puts)	- Premium	= Sales Proceeds
$50,000	- $7,000	= $43,000

For tax purposes, Morty will report sales proceeds of $43,000 and a cost basis of $38,000.

24. **(A)**

Let's start by reviewing how the premium is calculated on the Japanese Yen:

Premium (move decimal FOUR places to the left)	X Contract Size	X Number of Contracts	= $ Premium received for writing options
.000417	X 1,000,000	X 3	= $1,251

Premium (move decimal FOUR places to the left)	X Contract Size	X Number of Contracts	= $ Premium paid for purchasing options
.000311	X 1,000,000	X 3	= $933

Note, we first must move the decimal point on the premium FOUR places to the left. Additionally, the contract size of the Japanese Yen is 1,000,000. The Japanese Yen is the exception on the Series 7 exam. All other foreign currencies require the decimal point on the premium to be moved TWO places to the left, and the contract sizes are 10,000.

The investor earns a profit of $318 which can be expressed as follows:

Type of Transaction	Transaction	Premium
Opening Sale	Wrote 3 XDN Oct 120 puts	+$1,251 (credit)
Closing Purchase	Bought 3 XDN Oct 120 puts	-$933 (debit)
+$318 Profit		

25. **(D)**

The investor has purchased a Combination. As a combination buyer, the investor is long both a call and a put on the same security with different expiration dates and/or strike prices. A Combination buyer always has two breakeven points, which are calculated in the following manner:

Strike Price of call option	+ Total Premium	= Upside Breakeven
25	+ 5	= 30

Strike Price of put option	- Total Premium	= Downside Breakeven
20	- 5	= 15

It is important to add that a combination buyer expects "volatility". So, if asked, the investor would state the following: "Between now and expiration of the options, I expect DEF stock to trade above $30 or below $15."

26. **(A)**

The regulation T requirement for the purchase of puts (or calls) is 100%. In other words, the investor is required to pay in full and is not extended any credit.

27. **(A)**

Stacy has written a straddle, which means she is short both a call and a put on the same security, expiration dates, and strike prices. A straddle writer always has two breakeven points which are calculated in the following manner:

Strike Price of call option	+ Total Premium	= Upside Breakeven
35	+ 3	= 38

Strike Price of put option	- Total Premium	= Downside Breakeven
35	- 3	= 32

It is important to add that a straddle writer expects "neutrality" or "lack of volatility". Stated another way, straddle writers are neither bullish nor bearish, but expect the stock to stay in a narrow range. So, if asked, Stacy would state the following: "Between now and expiration of the options, I expect XYZ stock to stay within the range of $38/share and $32/share. In other words, I don't expect XYZ stock to go above $38 or below $32/share.

28. **(A)**

The investor has created a Put Spread. By purchasing an ABC Mar 55 Put for 5 and writing an ABC Mar 50 put for 3, she has a net debit of 2 points. In other words, the investor received more money than has been paid out, establishing a net debit of 2 points.

To determine the breakeven point, utilize the following steps:

1. Determine the dominant leg of the spread; this is the put option with the higher premium, which is the Mar 55 put.
2. Strike price from the dominant leg – net debit, 55 – 2 = 53

The breakeven is $53/share. At $53/share the Mar 55 put that the investor purchased has 2 points of intrinsic value and the investor could purchase the stock in the market and exercise the Mar 55 put, selling the stock at a 2-point profit. The 2-point profit would then be offset against the initial net debit established of 2 points. The investor does not make or lose money.

29. **(C)**

Adam has created a Bullish Vertical Debit Call Spread. We will begin by rewriting the position as follows:

Transactions
Bought 1 ABC Oct 65 Call *(dominant position)*
Sold 1 ABC Oct 70 Call

Even though premiums are not provided in the question, the call option with the lower strike would have a larger premium. We can now focus our attention on the call option with the lower strike price or higher premium. Since Adam has bought the ABC Oct 65 call, he would have a net debit. In addition, the purchase of the Oct 65 call would also be bullish.

30. **(A)**

Since an executed agreement is not received within the allotted time (15 days of account approval by a Registered Options Principal), the customer may only engage in closing transactions. Since the position was opened with the sale of 3 XYZ Sept 60 calls at, he may only engage in a closing purchase, or liquidate his existing position.

31. **(A)**

This is an example of a spread, which consists of the purchase and sale of puts or calls on the same security, which may have the same or different expiration dates or strike prices. This depends on the type of spread (vertical, horizontal, or diagonal spread).

32. **(B)**

Mr. William's has engaged in a Covered Put Writing Strategy. Let us now take a closer look at the position:

Transaction	Outlook
Short 100 shares of DEF at $50	Bearish
Short 1 DEF Feb 45 puts at 2	Bullish

Overall Mr. Williams is bearish, as his dominant position is the short sale as a result of having more money positioned on that side. His maximum gain will be realized when DEF stock declines. However, he will not profit from $50 (short sale price) down to zero as he will receive an assignment notice on the put option. The result of the stock declining below $45 (exercise price of the put) is:

Transaction	Debit or Credit
Short 100 shares of DEF at $50	+$5,000 credit
Short 1 DEF Feb 45 puts at 2	+$200 credit
Assignment of put – obligation to buy 100 shares of DEF at $45	-$4,500 debit
+$700 profit	

33. **(B)**

An options premium is composed of intrinsic value + time value. Even though we do not know the price at which PWE stock is trading, the put option with the lowest strike price would also have the smallest premium. If Bruce were to purchase an June 70 put, this option would give him the right to sell 100 shares of PWE stock at $70.

34. **(B)**

The most Zack can lose as a buyer of call options is the premium or debit paid. Zack paid a premium of 3, which is calculated as follows:

Premium (move decimal TWO places to the left)	X Contract Size	X Number of Contracts	= $Premium
.03	X 10,000	X 2	$600

Note, we first must move the decimal point on the premium TWO places to the left. Additionally, the contract size of the British Pound is 10,000. On all foreign currencies tested on the Series 7 exam with the exception of the Japanese Yen, we move the decimal point on the premium TWO places to the left, and the contract sizes are 10,000.

35. **(B)**

Writing call options is a bearish strategy as the writer would like the call options to trade at or below the strike price at expiration, so the calls would expire worthless.

Since the question does not indicate that Hale owns the stock, he has written uncovered or naked call options. As a result, he is subject to unlimited loss potential. Theoretically, the Swiss Franc could rise to infinity. The call options would be exercised by the buyer. This means that as the writer of naked calls, Hale would receive an assignment notice which would trigger the obligation to sell Swiss Francs at the strike price. Since Hale does not own Swiss Francs, he would first need to go out to the market to purchase Swiss Francs in the market at an infinite price and then sell Swiss Francs to the buyer at the strike price.

36. **(C)**

Robert has created a Bullish Debit Call Spread. We will begin by rewriting the position as follows:

Transactions
Bought 1 ABC Oct 65 Call *(**dominant position**)*
Sold 1 ABC June 70 Call

Even though premiums are not given in the question, the call option with the lower strike and longer expiration would have a larger premium. We can now focus our attention on the call option with the higher premium. Since Robert has purchased an ABC Oct 65 call, he has created a net debit. In addition, the purchase of the Oct 65 call would also be a bullish strategy.

37. **(D)**

Note this is an "except" question. One disadvantage of purchasing a put option over selling APPL stock short is that an option has a finite life or expiration date. The investor must be accurate in the timeframe that the stock declines since a standard option expires within a maximum of 9 months.

38. **(A)**

Any listed option that exceeds nine months until expiration are called Long-Term AnticiPation Securities ("LEAPS"). LEAPS are initially issued with a 39-month expiration and have January expiration dates. Other than the differences just discussed, LEAPS have a contract size of 100 shares just like standard options.

The premium is calculated as follows:

Premium	X Contract Size	X Number of Contracts	= $Premium
14	X 100	X 5	$7,000

The customer's total purchase price is $7,000.

39. **(A)**

The customer has created a Covered Put Writing strategy, which in this context does not imply safety. Covered means covered for margin purposes whereby there is no additional margin requirement deposit on the sale of the 5 XOM Sept 80 puts that the customer has written for a premium of 3. The cash deposit is calculated as follows:

50% of Short Sale Proceeds	- Premium	= Cash deposit
$18,750	- $1,500	= $17,250

The investor is required to deposit $17,250, after which the investor will have met the margin requirement of $18,750 since the premium of $1,500 is in the account for writing the puts.

40. **(B)**

The position is a Protective Put Purchase, which consists of a long stock position and a long put.

Hale buys 1 AT&T put option only as an insurance policy to protect against a decline in his long AT&T stock position. The breakeven point per share is the initial stock price plus the premium paid for the put. So, first we need to calculate the breakeven point. Hale needs AT&T stock to rise to $33/share to recoup the 3-point premium paid for the put. So, at $33/share, Hale's AT&T stock, which was purchased at $30/share, is sold at $33/share resulting in a 3-point profit. The 3-point profit on the sale of the stock is offset against the 3-point premium paid for the put options. The result is the breakeven point.

A profit is generated when the stock trades higher than $33/share. At $34/share, Hale makes a profit of 4 points on the stock. The puts expire worthless, resulting in a loss of 3 points. Netting out the 4-point profit on the stock and the 3-point loss on the put results in an overall profit of 1-point.

41. **(C)**

Alice would lose her entire premium if XYZ stock is trading at or below its strike price at expiration. An option is only worth its intrinsic value or in-the-money amount at expiration. If XYZ stock trades below the strike price of the May 35 call, the option would be out-of-the-money (I) and have zero intrinsic value. If XYZ stock trades at the strike price of the May 35 call, the option would be at-the-money (II) and would also have zero intrinsic value.

42. **(A)**

Broad-based index options trade each day until 4:15pm eastern time. Broad-based indices such as the S&P 500, Russell 2000, and Nasdaq 100 are examples of broad-based index options as they are diversified across industry lines.

Narrow-based index options trade each day until 4:00pm eastern time and are limited to one commodity or sector of the market. Examples include: CBOE Oil Index options, CBOE Gold Index options, and CBOE Internet Index options.

43. **(C)**

Since the investor exercises the call option in his cash account, he is required to deposit the aggregate exercise price which is calculated as follows:

Strike Price	X Number of Contracts	X Contract Size	= $Aggregate Exercise Price
50	X 1	X 100	= $5,000

Note, the premium of $300 is a separate transaction that was already paid out of the investor's account, and is Not subtracted from the aggregate exercise price.

44. **(C)**

The SPX June 1240 index put is in-the-money or has an intrinsic value of 15 points. Index options are cash settled, which means that the writer is required to pay the buyer the intrinsic value of 15 points upon exercise, which is calculated as follows:

Intrinsic value or In-the-Money Amount (points0	X Number of Contracts	X Contract Size	= $Intrinsic value
15	X 1	X 100	= $1,500

45. **(D)**

As the writer of a put, Zack is bullish on LMN stock. If exercised by the buyer, Zack would be obligated to purchase 100 shares of LMN at $30, hence establishing a long position in LMN. The position also has limited risk which can be expressed as follows:

Aggregate Exercise Price	-	Premium	= $Maximum Loss
$3,000	-	$300	= $2,700

As we see, the maximum loss is limited to $2,700. Zack could be obligated to purchase the stock for $3,000. If the stock declined to zero, Zack would lose his $3,000 less the premium received of $300.

46. **(B)**

A spread consists of a purchase AND sale. As a result, we can eliminate choices A and D as they combine either two purchases or two sales. To create a debit spread, we would purchase the call option with the lower strike price. Since the expiration dates are the same, the call option with the lower strike price would have a larger premium since it gives the holder the right to buy the stock at a lower price.

47. **(D)**

You should be able to identify the position as a Long Straddle. The straddle buyer is long both a call and a put on the same security, expiration dates, and strike prices. He expects "volatility" in the underlying security. Stated another way, straddle buyers are neither bullish nor bearish, but expect the stock to fluctuate in a wide range.

Let's take a closer look at the example:

The investor buys 1 KO June 65 straddle at 7.75. He has two breakeven points: 72.75 and 57.25 (strike price of call + premium and the strike price of the put – premium). As a straddle buyer, the investor expects the stock to trade above $72.25/share or below $57.25/share. He needs a large move in the stock either to the upside or downside to recoup the total premium paid for the call and put.

48. **(A)**

Selling a naked or uncovered call option is subject to unlimited risk. Theoretically, the underlying stock could rise to infinity. The call option would be exercised by the buyer. This means the call writer would receive an assignment notice which would trigger the obligation to sell the stock at the strike price. Since the call writer does not own the underlying security, it would first need to be purchased in the market at an infinite price and then sold at the strike price.

49. **(A)**

Jack paid a premium of $1,500 for his put options which can be expressed as follows:

Premium	X Contract Size	X number of contracts	= $premium
3	X 100	X 5	= $1,500

Jack does not lose any money on the value of his stock position since the value remains unchanged.

50. **(D)**

The breakeven point can be expressed as follows:

Strike Price of Put	- Premium	= Breakeven Point per share
40	- 7	= 33

The investor has a breakeven point of $33/share. It is important to note, both the buyer and the writer break even at the same price. At $33/share, the writer would be obligated to buy the stock at the strike price of $40/share. The writer would lose $7/share upon receiving the assignment notice which would be offset against the premium initially received.

OPTIONS EXAM 9

1. A customer purchases 1 PFE July 25 put at 3 when the market price of the stock is at $23. At expiration, the maximum potential loss is:

   (A) $300
   (B) $2,800
   (C) $2,500
   (D) $2,200

2. An investor is long a GHI Mar 65 put. The addition of which of the following positions would create a bear spread? Short a GHI Mar:

   (A) 60 put
   (B) 70 put
   (C) 60 call
   (D) 70 call

3. Bobby buys 1 LNP Mar 45 put at 3 and also buys 1 LNP Mar 50 call at 4.5. At which of the following prices will Bobby break even?

   I. $57.50
   II. $54.50
   III. $37.50
   IV. $42

   (A) I and III
   (B) I and IV
   (C) II and III
   (D) II and IV

4. An investor buys an HD May 35 call for 5 and also buys an HD May 30 put for 3. The stock declines to $27, and the call expires worthless. The investor buys 100 shares of HD at the market and exercises the put. What is the resulting profit or loss?

   (A) $300 profit
   (B) $800 loss
   (C) $600 profit
   (D) $500 loss

5. An investor goes long 1 ABC June 40 put at 7. What is his maximum potential gain?

   (A) $4,700
   (B) Unlimited
   (C) $3,300
   (D) $700

6. An investor is long an IBM Apr 135 put. The addition of which of the following positions would create a long straddle?

   (A) Short an IBM Apr 135 put
   (B) Short an IBM Apr 135 call
   (C) Long an IBM Apr 135 put.
   (D) Long an IBM Apr 135 call

7. Tony writes 10 XYZ Oct 30 calls at 3.50, and also writes 10 XYZ Oct 30 puts at 3. What is Tony's maximum gain?

   (A) $6,500
   (B) Unlimited
   (C) $3,500
   (D) $3,000

8. An investor writes 2 LXO June 65 calls and simultaneously buys 2 LXO June 70 calls. Which two of the following are correct?

   I.   Credit spread
   II. Debit spread
   III. He expects the spread to narrow
   IV. He expects the spread to widen

   (A) I and III
   (B) I and IV
   (C) II and III
   (D) II and IV

9. Barry holds a long position in IBM stock. Which one of the following option strategies would best protect his long stock position?

   (A) Writing IBM puts
   (B) Buying IBM puts
   (C) Writing IBM calls
   (D) Buying IBM calls

10. Victor purchases an ABC Dec 60 call for $700 when the underlying stock is trading at $63. What is the time value of the call option?

(A) $400
(B) $700
(C) $300
(D) $0

11. In which two of the following situations could an investor be positioned to acquire a long stock position? The investor is:

I.   long a put option
II. short a put option
III. long a call option
IV. short a call option

(A) I and III
(B) I and IV
(C) II and III
(D) II and IV

12. On the day prior to expiration, the Options Clearing Corporation (OCC) will automatically exercise an option for a customer if it is in-the-money by how much?

(A) .25 point
(B) .125 point
(C) 1 point
(D) .50 point

13. Dominick buys a DEF Feb 35 put at 6. Which two of the following best describe this strategy?

I.   Bullish strategy
II. Bearish strategy
III. Limited loss potential
IV. Unlimited loss potential

(A) I and III
(B) I and IV
(C) II and III
(D) II and IV

14. A credit put spread can be created from which two of the following?

I.   Long 1 JNJ Oct 80 put
II. Short 1 JNJ Oct 80 put
III. Long 1 JNJ Oct 85 put
IV. Short 1 JNJ Oct 85 put

(A) I and IIII
(B) I and IV
(C) II and III
(D) II and IV

15. Ralph expects XOM stock to depreciate significantly over the next few months. He would like to position himself to take advantage of this decline, but would also like to limit his risk. As Ralph's registered rep, which of the following strategies would be most consistent with Ralph's objective? Establish a:

(A) short position in XOM stock
(B) long position in XOM puts
(C) bearish vertical debit spread
(D) long straddle

16. Which strategy entails the greatest risk?

(A) A short sale of 500 shares of ABC stock at $65 and the purchase of 5 ABC June 70 calls at 3.25.
(B) A short sale of 500 shares of ABC stock at $65 and the sale of 5 ABC June 60 puts at 3.
(C) The purchase of 500 shares of ABC stock at $65 and the purchase of 5 ABC 60 puts at 3.
(D) The purchase of 500 shares of ABC stock at $65 and the sale of 5 ABC June 70 calls at 3.25.

17. An investor is long 1 FGH Aug 35 call. The addition of which of the following positions would create a credit spread? Write 1:

(A) FGH Aug 35 call
(B) FCH Aug 30 call
(C) FGH Aug 40 call
(D) FGH Aug 30 call

18. Todd goes long 5 XON Oct 75 puts at a premium of 7. With the stock trading at $77, how much time value do the put options have?

    (A) 7 points
    (B) 5 points
    (C) 0 points
    (D) -2 points

19. If the holder of a put option decided to exercise his option, he would ultimately have which of the following positions?

    (A) Short stock position
    (B) Long stock position
    (C) No position
    (D) Hedged position

20. The AMZN Sept 140 put would be out-of-the-money if the underlying stock was trading at which of the following prices?

    (A) 140
    (B) 137
    (C) 139.75
    (D) 142.25

21. Susan is looking for a strategy with unlimited potential gain. Which of the following strategies is consistent with her objective?

    (A) Writing calls
    (B) Buying calls
    (C) Writing puts
    (D) Buying puts

22. Hank buys 200 shares of OE at $30, and also purchases 2 OE July 20 puts at 2. What is Hank's maximum potential loss?

    (A) $400
    (B) $2,000
    (C) $2,400
    (D) $1,200

23. A customer purchases a TOP Feb 60 call at 4 and sells a TOP Feb 55 call at 6. The customer would earn a profit in all of the following scenarios EXCEPT:

    (A) Both calls expire worthless
    (B) The spread narrows
    (C) The spread widens
    (D) TOP common stock declines sharply

24. Howie wrote a GIG Dec 65 call at 6. What is Howie's maximum potential loss?

    (A) $7,100
    (B) Unlimited
    (C) $600
    (D) $5,900

25. An investor establishes the following position:

    Long 100 XOM stock at $75
    Long 1 XOM Aug 70 put at 3
    Short 1 XOM Aug 80 call at 4

    What is the investor's maximum loss?

    (A) $7,400
    (B) $400
    (C) Unlimited
    (D) $800

26. The term "exercise price" is synonymous with which of the following?

    (A) Strike price
    (B) Premium
    (C) Contract size
    (D) Transaction price

27. Edwin bought 100 shares of IBM at $65 and sold 1 IBM Apr 70 call at 3. At what price would Edwin break even?

    (A) $68
    (B) $67
    (C) $73
    (D) $62

28. An investor buys 1,000 ABC at $50/share, and also writes 10 ABC Sept 55 calls at 3. What is the investor's margin requirement?

    (A) $25,000
    (B) $28,000
    (C) $53,000
    (D) $22,000

29. A customer expects GS stock to trade over a narrow price range over the next few months. Which of the following strategies would be consistent with the customer's expectation?

    (A) Long Straddle
    (B) Short Combination
    (C) Horizontal Spread
    (D) Vertical Spread

30. An investor is bullish on Whole Foods stock. Which two of the following strategies would you recommend?

    I.   Long puts
    II. Short puts
    III. Long calls
    IV. Short calls

    (A) I and III
    (B) I and IV
    (C) II and III
    (D) II and IV

31. A customer writes 1 JKL May 55 call at 2 when JKL stock is trading at $52/share. What is the customer's margin requirement?

    (A) $720
    (B) $520
    (C) $1,040
    (D) $940

32. A customer would like to begin trading options. When must the account be approved for trading options?

    (A) No later than the time the first order is accepted by the RR
    (B) Before the first order is accepted
    (C) Within 15 of placing the first order
    (D) 15 days prior to placing the first order

33. An investor buys 1 XYZ June 65 call and also buys 1 XYZ June 60 put. What is the name of this strategy?

    (A) Combination
    (B) Straddle
    (C) Vertical Spread
    (D) Diagonal Spread

34. Gary buys 10 XYZ Oct 30 calls at 3.50, and also buys 10 XYZ Oct 30 puts at 3. What is Gary's maximum loss?

    (A) Unlimited
    (B) $3,000
    (C) $3,500
    (D) $6,500

35. Todd goes long 5 XON Oct 75 puts at a premium of 7. With the stock trading at $73 per share, how much time value do the put options have?

    (A) 7 points
    (B) 5 points
    (C) 0 points
    (D) 2 points

36. An investor placed the following trades in his margin account:

    Buy 100 PQR common stock at $40
    Sell short 100 TUV common stock at $60
    Sell 1 PQR Apr 40 call at 3.
    Sell 1 TUV May 60 put at 5.

    What is investor's margin requirement?

    (A) $5,800
    (B) $5,000
    (C) $4,200
    (D) $10,800

37. An investor writes 2 XYZ Nov 30 calls at 2. Which one of the following statements best describes the investor's outlook? The investor is bearish and has:

    (A) an unlimited potential maximum gain.
    (B) a potential maximum gain of $400.
    (C) a potential maximum gain of $2,000.
    (D) a potential maximum gain of $200.

38. Ted goes short 3 FED Aug 50 puts at 2. What is Ted's maximum potential gain?

    (A) $14,400
    (B) $15,000
    (C) $600
    (D) $200

39. Which of the following option strategies does Not have limited gain potential?

    (A) Short put
    (B) Long put
    (C) Long call
    (D) Short call

40. Sandy goes short 3 PFE Apr 45 puts at 3 and also goes short 3 PFE Apr 45 calls at 4. At what price does the underlying stock need to trade for Sandy to generate a profit?

    (A) $52
    (B) $51.25
    (C) $37.50
    (D) $38

41. Which two of the following are bearish spreads?

    I.   Net debit vertical call spread
    II. Net credit vertical call spread
    III. Net debit vertical put spread
    IV. Net credit vertical put spread

    (A) I and III
    (B) I and IV
    (C) II and III
    (D) II and IV

42. Mr. Halasi writes 1 naked JKL June 65 put at 3. What is his maximum loss?

    (A) Premium
    (B) Unlimited
    (C) The aggregate exercise + premium received
    (D) The aggregate exercise price - premium received

43. A customer has established the following position in his account:

    Bought 1 T-Bond call option

    What is the customer's expectation? He expects:

    (A) interest rates to increase.
    (B) interest rates to decline.
    (C) interest rates to stay in a narrow range.
    (D) interest rates to fluctuate in a wide range.

44. An investor buys 500 shares of JNJ common stock at $80/share and also writes 5 JNJ May 85 calls at 4. Which two of the following would be the correct way to mark the options order ticket?

    I.   Closing sale
    II. Opening sale
    III. Covered
    IV. Uncovered

    (A) I and III
    (B) I and IV
    (C) II and III
    (D) II and IV

45. Seven months ago, a customer of Big Capital LLC sold short 100 shares of GHI stock at $50/share, and also wrote a GHI Nov 50 put for 6. What is the purpose of writing this put option?

    (A) His position now has limited risk
    (B) This is an income-generating strategy
    (C) He is moderately bullish
    (D) He has created a hedge

46. A customer has established the following position in his account:

    Bought 1 T-Bond put option

    What is the customer's expectation?

    (A) Interest rates to decline
    (B) Interest rates to increase
    (C) Interest rates to fluctuate in a wide range
    (D) Interest rates to stay in a narrow range

47. What is the contract size for Euro options?

    (A) 100
    (B) 1,000
    (C) 10,000
    (D) 1,000,000

48. A speculator believes that the U.S. dollar will strengthen against the Japanese Yen over the next three months. Which of the following would be the appropriate position to take to benefit from his expectation?

    (A) Long U.S. dollar put options
    (B) Short U.S. dollar put options
    (C) Short Japanese Yen put options
    (D) Long Japanese Yen put options

49. Which one of the following formulas can be used to determine the time value of an option? Time value is equal to the premium:

    (A) minus intrinsic value.
    (B) plus intrinsic value.
    (C) times intrinsic value.
    (D) divided by intrinsic value.

50. What are the characteristics of purchasing a put option?

    I.   Bullish
    II. Bearish
    III. Limited risk
    IV. Unlimited risk

    (A) I and III
    (B) I and IV
    (C) II and III
    (D) II and IV

OPTIONS EXPLANATIONS 9

1. **(A)**

The maximum potential loss is always limited to the premium paid of $300 and is calculated as follows:

Premium	X Contract Size	X Number of Contracts	= $Premium
3	X 100	X 1	= $300

2. **(A)**

The investor is already long (bought) a GHI Mar 65 put. By writing the GHI Mar 60 put (lower strike price) would allow the investor to maintain his bearish position. Since the investor purchased the put with the higher strike price (dominant leg) he is bearish. The two choices that contain calls can be eliminated (Choices C & D). Spreads either contain calls OR puts, but not both.

3. **(A)**

You should be able to identify the position as a Long Combination. The combination buyer is long both a call and a put on the same security, with different expiration dates and/or strike prices. And like the straddle buyer, the combination buyer expects "volatility" in the underlying security. Stated another way, combination buyers are neither bullish nor bearish, but expect the stock to fluctuate in a wide range. Let's take a closer look at Bobby's position:

Strike Price of Call	+ Total Premium	= Upside Breakeven Point
50	+ 7.5	= 57.5

Strike Price of Put	- Total Premium	= Downside Breakeven Point
45	- 7.5	= 37.5

Bobby will break even if LNP trades up to $57.50 or down to 37.50 by expiration. He will earn a profit if the stock trades above or below his breakeven points.

4. **(D)**

The transactions result in a loss of $500, which can be determined as follows:

Transaction	Debit or Credit
Bought an HD May 35 call for 5	-$500 debit
Bought an HD may 30 put for 3	-$300 debit
Bought 100 HD at $27	-2,700 debit
Exercise of put (obligation to sell 100 shares of HD at $30)	+$3,000 credit
-$500 loss	

5. **(C)**

As the buyer of a put, the investor's maximum potential gain would be realized if the stock declined to zero. If the market for ABC fell to zero, the investor could buy the stock at $0/share and exercise his put, selling the stock to the writer at the strike price of $40/share. The investor's profit would be 40 points less the 7 point premium paid for the put or $700. To summarize, the maximum gain for the purchaser of a put can be determined as follows:

Aggregate Exercise Price	-	Premium	= Maximum Gain
$4,000	-	700	= $3,300

6. **(D)**

The investor has created a Long Straddle with the purchase of (long) an IBM Apr 135 call. The straddle buyer is long both a call and a put on the same security, expiration dates, and strike prices. The straddle buyer expects "volatility" in the underlying security. Stated another way, straddle buyers are neither bullish nor bearish, but expect the stock to fluctuate in a wide range.

7. **(A)**

You should be able to identify Tony's position as a short straddle (straddle writer). The straddle writer is short both a call(s) and a put(s) on the same security, expiration dates, strike prices. The maximum gain for Tony (or any straddle writer) would be the total premium received for writing the straddle. The total premium is 6.50. The dollar amount can be determined as follows:

Total Premium	X number of contracts	X contract size	= $Premium
6.50	X 10	X 100	= $6,500

Ideally, at expiration, Tony would like the stock to be exactly at $30/share. At $30/share, both the calls and the puts are at-the-money and would expire worthless. Tony would then keep the total premium received without having either the put or call assigned to him.

8. **(A)**

The first step is being able to identify that this is a credit spread. Even though no premiums are given, you can determine that the call option with the Lower Strike Price has a higher premium (since the expiration dates are the same).

The investor writes or sells the 65 call which brings in more money that is paid out for the 70 call. As a result, the investor is a "net seller" or has established a credit spread. Ideally a net seller or writer would like both options to expire worthless.

Let us expand on this by utilizing some hypothetical numbers. The investor sold the 65 call for a premium of 5 and bought the 70 call for 3. The investor would have a net credit of 2. The goal of a net creditor or writer would be for the option to expire worthless. In other words, he would like the spread to go to zero by expiration. If the spread was established at a net credit of 2 and expires at zero, the spread is said to narrow; go from a higher number to a lower number.

9. **(B)**

The purchase of puts on IBM stock would create a Protective Put Purchase. Barry would utilize the long puts as only as an insurance policy to protect against a decline in his long IBM stock position. In a worst case scenario, IBM stock declines to $0/share, and Barry exercises his put options and sells IBM stock at the strike price of the put option. For example, if the strike price of the IBM put is 160, Barry would sell his IBM stock at the strike price, not the market price of $0/share.

Choice C would create a covered call option, which would not protect Barry against a sharp decline in the market price of IBM stock. The premium received from the call option would only provide a slight cushion that would not protect Barry from a severe decline in the stock.

Choices A and D are both bullish option positions. Both writing puts and buying calls would increase Barry's risk since these positions are on the same side of the market (bullish) as his stock position.

10. **(A)**

Here is the method for determining the Time Value of an option:

Option Premium	-	Intrinsic Value	= Time Value

So, first we need to determine if the option has any intrinsic value or money value. A call option is in-the-money if the exercise price or strike price is below the market price of the underlying stock. Since the exercise price is below the market price, the option has 3 points or $300 of intrinsic value. Now let us go back to our example:

Option Premium	-	Intrinsic Value	= Time Value
$700	-	300	=$400

The key is to always determine whether or not an option has intrinsic value or money value first before attempting to determine if an option has time value. Whatever amount remains is the time value.

11. **(C)**

An investor that is short a put or long a call is positioned to acquire a long stock position. An investor that is short a put or a put writer would be obligated to purchase the stock at the strike price, therefore acquiring a long position. An investor that is long a call has the right to buy the underlying stock, therefore also acquiring a long position.

12. **(A)**

On the day prior to expiration, the OCC will automatically exercise an option if it is in-the-money by at least .25 (1/4) point. The OCC will automatically exercise an option for a broker-dealer's account if it is in-the-money by at least .125 (1/8) of a point.

13. **(C)**

The purchase of a put has limited gain potential. Dominick is bearish as the purchaser of a put. He can only profit from the strike price (35) to zero, less the premium paid. If DEF stock fell to zero, Dominick could purchase the stock at zero, and exercise his put which would allow him to sell his stock at $35/share. He would then make a profit of 35 points less the 6 point premium.

14. **(B)**

A credit put spread can be created with the following two positions:

| Long 1 JNJ Oct 80 put | Debit |
| Short 1 JNJ Oct 85 put | Credit (dominant leg) |

Even though premiums are not given in the question, the Oct 85 Put would have a higher premium (dominant leg) given the same expiration dates. Going short (selling or writing) the Oct 85 put would result in receiving more premium than the premium paid (debit) for purchasing the Oct 80 put, resulting in a net credit.

15. **(B)**

Establishing a long position in XOM puts would be most consistent with Ralph's objective. While all four choices should benefit from a significant decline in XOM stock, not all positions are consistent with Ralph's objective of limited risk. For example, a short position in XOM stock (Choice A) would subject Ralph to unlimited risk should the XOM stock rise. While a bearish vertical debit spread (Choice C) would limit risk, the potential profit is also limited to the difference between the two strike prices less the premium paid. A long straddle (Choice D) would be consistent with the expectation of volatility as opposed to a bearish outlook. A long position in XOM puts (Choice B) would be best as the risk is limited to the premium paid, and the potential profit is significant as Ralph could from the strike price down to zero, less the premium paid.

16. **(B)**

Choice B, short stock and a short put is a Covered Put Writing strategy which entails unlimited risk, as the stock could theoretically rise to infinity. The unlimited risk arises from the short stock position. The short put would only provide protection limited to the premium received. The term "covered" in this context is misleading and does not mean 'safe". It means covered for margin purposes as the margin requirement would be limited to 50% of the short sale. No margin requirement is imposed on the sale of the put option. The other three strategies entail limited risk a follows:

- Choice A – Protective Call Purchase
- Choice C – Protective Put Purchase
- Choice D – Covered Call Writing

17. **(D)**

A credit spread would be created by writing 1 FGH Aug 30 call. If the investor writes or sells an FGH Aug 30 call, this will bring more money that is paid out for purchase of the FGH Aug 35 call. The call option with the Lower Strike Price (given the same expiration date) would have a higher premium. As a result, the investor is a "net seller" or has established a credit spread. Ideally a net seller or writer would like both options to expire worthless.

18. **(A)**

Here is the method for determining the Time Value of an option:

Option Premium	- Intrinsic Value	= Time Value

So, first we need to determine if the option has an intrinsic value or money value. A put option is in-the-money if the exercise price or strike price is above the market price of the underlying stock. Since the exercise price is below the market price, the option has zero intrinsic value (there is no such thing as negative intrinsic value).

Let's go back to our example:

Option Premium (points)	- Intrinsic Value	= Time Value
7	- 0	= 7

The key is to always determine whether or not an option has intrinsic value or money value first before attempting to determine if an option has time value. Whatever amount remains is the time value.

19. **(A)**

When the holder (buyer) of a put exercises his option, he is exercising his right to sell the stock. Based upon the limited information provided in the question, we can assume the investor does not own the stock. As a result, selling stock that the investor does not own would create or saddle the investor with a short stock position.

20. **(D)**

The AMZN Sept 140 put would be out-of-the money or have zero intrinsic value if the market price of the stock (142.25) was above the exercise price. So, if the investor wanted to sell 100 shares of AMZN stock, it would be better to sell the stock at the market price of $142.25/share then to exercise his put, selling the stock at 140 (strike price).

21. **(B)**

Buying call options has unlimited potential gain as the buyer has the right to purchase the underlying security at the strike price. Theoretically, the underlying security could rise to infinite price in which the buyer could then sell the security.

Buying puts (Choice D) has limited gain potential has the underlying security can only decline to zero. The put buyer's profit is limited to the difference between the strike price and zero less the premium paid. Writing calls and puts (Choices A and C) have a maximum gain limited to the premium or credit received.

22. **(C)**

The position is a Protective Put Purchase, which consists of a long stock position and a long put(s). Hank is using the long puts as an insurance policy to protect against a decline in his long OE stock position. His maximum loss will be realized when the underlying stock trades $20/share or lower. For example, if OE stock were to decline to zero, the result would be a loss of $2,400 which can be expressed as follows:

Transaction	Debit or Credit
Purchase Price of OE stock	-$6,000 debit
Premium Paid for OE Put Options	-$400 debit
Exercise of OE Put Options	+$4,000 credit
Maximum Loss = $2,400	

Note, Hank could sell his 200 shares of OE stock at $20, Not zero. This would be accomplished by exercising his OE put options and selling his 200 shares of OE stock at the strike price of $20.

23. **(C)**

This is an Except question, which means three of the four choices are correct. We are looking for the incorrect answer. The first step is being able to identify that this is a credit spread. The investor writes or sells the TOP Feb 55 call for a premium of 6 which brings in more money that is paid out for the purchase of the 60 call, which a premium of 4 is paid out. As a result, the investor is a "net seller" or has established a credit spread. Ideally a net seller or writer would like both options to expire worthless.

24. **(B)**

Theoretically, the underlying stock could rise to infinity. The call option would be exercised by the buyer. This means that as the writer of a naked call, Howie would receive an assignment notice which would trigger the obligation to sell the stock at the strike price. Since Howie does not own the underlying stock, he would first need to go out to the market to purchase the stock in the market at an infinite price and then sell the stock to the buyer at the strike price.

25. **(B)**

As seen below, the long stock position is the "dominant position". The worst possible scenario would be the stock declining to zero where the maximum loss would be realized as follows:

Transaction	Gain or loss on position
Long 100 XOM stock at $75	-$7,500
Long 1 XOM Aug 70 put at 3	+$6,700
Short 1 XOM Aug 80 call at 4	+$400
Maximum Loss = -$400	

26. **(A)**

The term "exercise price" is synonymous with "strike price". You will see that the exam uses these two terms interchangeably. In the case of a call option, the holder has the right to buy the underlying (stock, currency, etc.) at the exercise price or strike price. This price is a fixed or pre-determined price determined by the Options Clearing Corporation ("OCC") at issuance. In the case of a put option, the holder has the right to sell ('put") the underlying (stock, currency, etc.) at the exercise price or strike price. This price is also a fixed or pre-determined price determined by the OCC.

27. **(D)**

Edwin has created a Covered Call Writing strategy. The formula for the breakeven point is as follows:

Stock Price	- Premium	= Breakeven Point
$65/share	- 3	= $62

Edwin would break even at $62/share. While he is moderately bullish on IBM stock, if the position moved against him, at $62/share, he would have a loss on the long stock position which would be equally offset against the 3-point premium received for writing the call option.

28. **(A)**

The investor has created a Covered Call Writing strategy. The investor's Regulation T margin requirement is 50% of the stock or $25,000. "Covered" in the context of margin means that no additional margin deposit is required on the sale of the call options.

29. **(B)**

A Short Combination would be consistent with the customer's expectation. As a Combination Writer, the customer is short both a call and a put on the same security with different expiration dates and/or strike prices. A Combination writer always has two breakeven points, which is calculated in the following manner:

Strike Price of call option	+ total premium	= upside breakeven point
Strike Price of put option	- total premium	= downside breakeven point

Combination writers are neither bullish nor bearish, but expect the stock to trade within the breakeven points.

30. **(C)**

The two bullish positions are long calls and short puts. A long call allows the holder to purchase the stock at the strike price, therefore benefiting as the stock goes up. The writer of a put (short put) is also holding a bullish position. If the put writer receives an assignment notice, he would be saddled with a long position. In other words, he would be obligated to purchase the stock at the exercise price, hence establishing a long position.

We can summarize bullish and bearish positions as follows:

Bullish Positions	Bearish Positions
Buying (long) calls	Buying (long) puts
Writing (short) puts	Writing (short) calls

31. **(D)**

The margin requirement for writing naked or uncovered options is the greater of the Basic Margin Requirement and the Minimum Margin Requirement. Let's review both margin requirements here:

Basic Margin Requirement			
Premium	+ (20% X current market value of the underlying stock)	- Out-of-the-money amount	= Basic Margin Requirement
$200	+ $1,040	- 300	= $940

Minimum Margin Requirement		
Premium	+ (10% X current market value of the underlying stock)	= Minimum Margin Requirement
$200	+ $520	= $720

The greater of the Basic and Minimum Requirement is $940.

32. **(A)**

The customer must be approved for options trading no later than the time the first order is accepted by the RR. In other words, the customer may be approved prior to the first trade, but no later than the time the first order is accepted.

33. **(A)**

This strategy is a Combination which consists of both purchases or sales of a call(s) and a put(s) on the same security with different expiration dates and/or strike prices. Like the buyer of a Straddle, the Combination buyer expects volatility in the underlying security.

34. **(D)**

You should be able to identify the position as a Long Straddle. The straddle buyer is long both a call and a put on the same security, expiration dates, and strike prices. Now Gary's maximum loss is limited to the total premium paid, which is $6,500 and can be determined as follows:

Premium	X number of contracts	X contract size	= $Premium
3.50 (call)	X 10	X 100	=$3,500
3 (put)	X 10	X 100	=$3,000
=$6,500 Total Premium			

35. **(B)**

Here is the method for determining the Time Value of an option:

Option Premium	-	Intrinsic Value	= Time Value

So, first we need to determine if the option has any intrinsic value or money value. A put option is in-the-money if the exercise price or strike price is above the market price of the underlying stock. Since the exercise price is above the market price, the option has two points of intrinsic value. Let's go back to our example:

Option Premium	-	Intrinsic Value	= Time Value
7 points	-	2 points	= 5 points

The key is to always determine whether or not an option has intrinsic value or money value before attempting to determine if an option has any time value. Whatever amount remains is the time value.

36. **(B)**

The four positions can be rearranged into two strategies with two different margin requirements. The key is grouping the two strategies together that have the same underlying security as follows:

Covered Call Writing
Buy 100 PQR common stock at $40
Sell 1 PQR Apr 40 call at 3
Margin Requirement = $2,000

The margin requirement on a Covered Call Writing strategy is 50% of the long stock position.

Covered Put Writing
Sell short 100 TUV common stock at $60
Sell 1 TUV May 60 put at 5
Margin Requirement = $3,000

The margin requirement on a covered put writing strategy is 50% of the short stock position. The margin requirement for both positions is $5,000.

37. **(B)**

An investor who writes naked or uncovered calls is bearish. The position has limited gain potential equal to the premium or credit received of $400 which can be determined as follows:

Premium	X number of contracts	X contract size	= $credit
2	X 2	X 100	=$400 credit (maximum gain)

38. **(C)**

Ted has written 3 puts. His maximum potential gain is limited to the premium or credit received of $600 which can be determined as follows:

Premium	X number of contracts	X contract size	= $credit
2	X 3	X 100	=$600 credit (maximum gain)

39. **(C)**

Read the question carefully. The question reads: "Which of the following option strategies does NOT have limited gain potential? In other words, which option strategy has unlimited gain potential.

Long call options have unlimited gain potential. Long puts have limited gain potential as the investor can only profit from the exercise price down to zero less the premium paid. Short calls and short puts have limited gain potential, as the maximum gain is limited to the premium received.

40. **(B)**

Sandy has written a straddle. As a straddle writer, Sandy is short both a call and a put on the same security, expiration dates, and strike prices. While the question wants to know where Sandy would generate a profit, we first need to calculate the breakeven points. A straddle writer always has two breakeven points, calculated in the following manner:

Strike Price of Call	+ Total Premium	= Upside Breakeven Point
45	+ 7	= 52

Strike Price of Put	- Total Premium	= Downside Breakeven Point
45	- 7	= 38

It is also important to add that the straddle writer expects the stock to stay within a narrow range. So, Sandy will earn a profit if the stock stays within the range of $52 and $38. Since $51.25/share is within the range of $52 to $38, this is where Sandy will earn a profit.

41. **(C)**

Bearish spreads include net credit vertical call spreads, and net debit vertical put spreads.

Let us illustrate with an example of each:

Example #1

Net Credit Vertical Call Spread	Debit or Credit
Bought 1 DO Apr 60 Call	Debit
Sold 1 DO Apr 55 Call	**Credit (dominant leg)**

Premiums are not necessary to illustrate the above example. The call option with the lower strike would have a higher premium. We can now focus our attention on the DO Apr 55 Call Option (higher premium). Since the investor sold the DO Apr 55 call, he is bearish. Our dominant leg will always determine if the investor is bullish or bearish.

Example #2

Net Credit Vertical Put Spread	Debit or Credit
Bought 1 DO Apr 60 Put	**Debit (dominant leg)**
Sold 1 DO Apr 55 Put	Credit

The put option with the higher strike would have a higher premium. We can now focus our attention on the DO Apr 60 Put Option (higher premium). Since the investor bought the DO Apr 60 put, he is bearish. Again, our dominant leg will always determine if the investor is bullish or bearish.

42. **(D)**

As the writer of a put, Mr. Halasi is bullish on JKL stock. If exercised by the buyer, Mr. Halasi would be obligated to purchase 100 shares of JKL at $65, hence establishing a long position in JKL. The position also has limited risk which can be expressed as follows:

Aggregate Exercise Price	-	Premium	= $Maximum Loss
$6,500	-	$300	= $6,200

As we see the maximum loss is limited to $6,200. Mr. Halasi could be obligated to purchase the stock for $6,500. If the stock declines to zero, Mr. Halasi would lose his $6,500 less the premium received of $300 which he received.

43. **(B)**

The fundamental concepts of bonds apply to both T-bonds and T-bond options. Both T-bonds and T-bond options have an inverse relationship to interest rates. Since the customer purchased a T-bond call option, he expects T-bond prices to rise, and interest rates to decline.

44. **(C)**

Since the investor "initiated" the position with the sale of 5 JNJ May 85 calls, the ticket should be marked as an "Opening Sale". In addition, the investor has established a Covered Call Writing Strategy. The covered call writer owns (hence covered) the underlying stock. If the calls are exercised by the buyer (holder), the covered call writer will sell the stock that he already owns at the strike price (exercise price). So, the order ticket should be marked "covered".

45. **(B)**

The customer has created a Covered Put Writing strategy. Covered in this context does not imply safety. It means "covered for margin purposes" whereby there is no additional margin requirement deposit on the sale of the GHI Nov 50 put written for a premium of 3. However, the position has unlimited risk because of the short stock position. A Covered Put writing strategy is bearish as the dominant position is the short stock position. The put option is written to generate premium income.

46. **(B)**

The fundamental concepts of bonds apply to both T-bonds and T-bond options, which have an inverse relationship to interest rates. Since the customer purchased a T-bond put option, he expects T-Bond prices to decline and interest rates to increase.

47. **(C)**

On all foreign currencies tested on the Series 7 exam with one exception, the contract size is 10,000. The one exception is the Japanese Yen which is based on a contract size of 1 million.

48. **(D)**

The speculator anticipates that the U.S. dollar will strengthen against the Japanese. Stated another way, the speculator believes the Japanese Yen will weaken or decline in value. As a result, the speculator should assume a bearish position on the Japanese Yen, therefore establishing a long position in Japanese Yen Put Options.

Note on the Series 7 exam, never establish a position in U.S. dollar options even if it appears logical. The exam takes the position that U.S. dollar options do not exist, and you will be marked incorrect. Always assume the correct position in terms of foreign currency options.

49. **(A)**

Here is the method for determining the Time Value of an option:

Option Premium	- Intrinsic Value	= Time Value

The key is to always determine whether or not an option has intrinsic value or money value first before attempting to determine if an option has time value. Whatever amount remains is the time value.

50. **(C)**

The put buyer is bearish and is positioned to profit from a decline in the underlying security. Additionally, as a put buyer, the risk is limited to the premium or debit paid.

OPTIONS EXAM 10

1. An investor goes short an XYZ June 70 Straddle for a total premium of 6. All of the following are true statements EXCEPT:

   (A) the investor will earn a profit at $63
   (B) the investor will break even at $76
   (C) the investor would ideally like the stock to trade $70 at expiration
   (D) the investor had an initial credit of $600

2. According to Regulation T, when must a customer pay for the purchase of an option contract?

   (A) T + 5
   (B) Same day
   (C) T + 1
   (D) T + 3

3. A customer goes long an HRB Feb 25 call at 5. Shortly thereafter, the customer decides to exercise his option when the common stock is trading at $27/share. Which one of the following is correct? The customer has a:

   (A) $200 capital gain
   (B) $300 capital loss
   (C) $3,000 cost basis
   (D) $2,500 cost basis

4. Sally goes long 3 XYZ June 65 calls and also goes short 3 XYZ June 70 calls. What is the name of this strategy?

   (A) Horizontal Spread
   (B) Straddle
   (C) Vertical Spread
   (D) Diagonal Spread

5. S&P 500 Index options cease trading each day at:

   (A) 4:15pm eastern time
   (B) 4:00pm eastern time
   (C) 11:59pm eastern time
   (D) 5:30pm eastern time

6. Rick buys 1 MNO May 40 put and also buys 1 MNO May 45. What is this strategy called?

   (A) Combination
   (B) Diagonal spread
   (C) Vertical spread
   (D) Straddle

7. An investor writes 2 XYZ Nov 30 calls at 2. What is the investor's maximum potential gain?

   (A) Unlimited
   (B) $2,000
   (C) $200
   (D) $400

8. The premium of a yield-based call option is 3.25. This translates to a cost of:

   (A) $3,781.25
   (B) $3,78.13
   (C) $325
   (D) $3,250

9. Burt writes 1 XYZ Mar 65 put at 3 and also writes 1 XYZ Mar 60 call at 5. What is the name of this strategy?

   (A) Short combination
   (B) Short straddle
   (C) Vertical Spread
   (D) Diagonal

10. Raj owns 500 shares of MSFT stock which is currently trading at $25. Raj is moderately bullish on the stock over the next three to six months, and believes the stock has excellent long term prospects. His goal is to reduce his risk over the short term, and generate additional income in his portfolio. The addition of which of the following positions would help him accomplish this goal?

    (A) Sell 5 MSFT July 30 puts
    (B) Sell 5 MSFT July 30 calls
    (C) Buy 5 MSFT July 30 puts
    (D) Buy 5 MSFT July 30 calls

11. On July 7, 2010, Tara bought 1 NOX Feb 55 call at 8. On January 6, 2011, the NOX option expires worthless. For tax purposes, Tara has an $800:

    (A) short-term capital loss in 2010.
    (B) short-term capital loss in 2011.
    (C) long-term capital loss in 2010.
    (D) long-term capital loss in 2011.

12. On January 3, 2009, an investor buys 1,000 YUM stock at $35. On March 10, 2009 he sells 1,000 YUM stock at $28, realizing a $7,000 capital loss. Within thirty days, the purchase of which of the following would trigger a Wash Sale?

    (A) Sale of 10 YUM Sept 25 calls
    (B) Purchase of 10 YUM Sept 25 calls
    (C) Sale of 10 YUM Sept 25 puts
    (D) Purchase of 10 YUM Sept 25 puts

13. Which of the following strategies has the least degree of risk?

    (A) Sale of a straddle
    (B) Sale of a naked put
    (C) Short sale of stock
    (D) Sale of an uncovered call

14. Gary buys 10 XYZ Oct 30 calls at 3.50, and also buys 10 XYZ Oct 30 puts at 3. What is Gary's maximum potential gain?

    (A) Unlimited
    (B) $3,000
    (C) $3,500
    (D) $6,500

15. A portfolio manager in charge of an energy fund would like to protect his portfolio from a decline in the market. Utilizing options, which of the following would be the best way to protect his portfolio?

    (A) Buying narrow-based index put options
    (B) Writing narrow-based index call options
    (C) Buying broad-based index put options
    (D) Writing broad-based index call options

16. Greg buys 200 shares of ABC at $35 and also buys 2 ABC Feb 35 puts at 5. Following these purchases, negative news is announced and ABC stock declines to $22. Greg reacts to this by exercising his puts and liquidating his position. What is Greg's resulting profit or loss?

    (A) $500 loss
    (B) $1,000 loss
    (C) $1,800 loss
    (D) $3,600 loss

17. All of the following positions have unlimited gain potential Except:

    (A) Long stock + short put
    (B) Long stock + short call
    (C) Long call + long put
    (D) Long stock + long put

18. The premium minus intrinsic value is equal to the:

    (A) Exercise price
    (B) Market value
    (C) Time value
    (D) Money value

19. Steve buys 100 shares of RO at $45, and also purchases 1 RO Dec 45 put at 3. What is Steve's maximum potential loss?

    (A) $4,800
    (B) $4,200
    (C) $300
    (D) $4,500

20. Which one of the following is a correct statement regarding adjustment of an options contract for a "stock dividend"? The exercise price is:

    (A) decreased.
    (B) increased
    (C) unchanged
    (D) cancelled

21. A customer sells an RUT (Russell 2000 Index) Aug 800 put for 5. Five months later, the customer receives an assignment notice when the index settles at 785. What is the customer's obligation?

    (A) Pay the buyer $1,500 cash
    (B) Pay the buyer $2,000 cash
    (C) Deliver 100 shares of the RUT Index
    (D) Return the premium of $500 to the buyer

22. A customer contacts his broker-dealer to exercise his RIMM put option which trades on the CBOE. Who does his broker-dealer notify?

    (A) OCC
    (B) RIMM
    (C) CBOE
    (D) The contra broker

23. An investor established the following position in his options account:

    Bought 5 XOM Apr 75 calls at 4
    Sold 5 XOM Apr 70 calls at 7

    What is the investor's maximum loss?

    (A) $2,500
    (B) $1,000
    (C) Unlimited
    (D) $2,000

24. Carol sells short 1,000 ABC at $50, and goes long 10 ABC Dec 55 calls at 3. The following day, the stock rises to $62. Carol takes immediate action by exercising her calls when the stock is trading at $62/share. What is her resulting loss?

    (A) $5,000
    (B) $12,000
    (C) $15,000
    (D) $8,000

25. All of the following strategies have limited risk Except:

    (A) Writing a combination
    (B) Writing a covered call
    (C) Writing a naked put
    (D) Buying a straddle

26. A Canadian importer has agreed to make payments to its trading partner in U.S. dollars. Which two of the following will assist the Canadian exporter in hedging its position?

    I.   Buy Canadian Dollar calls
    II. Sell Canadian Dollar puts
    III. Buy Canadian Dollar puts
    IV. Sell Canadian Dollar calls

    (A) I and II
    (B) I and III
    (C) II and IV
    (D) III and IV

27. Tag Heuer (Swiss company) will be exporting watches to Target (U.S. company). Tag Heuer has agreed to accept payments in U.S. Dollars. How can Tag Heuer best protect its position?

    (A) Buy puts on the Swiss Franc
    (B) Buy calls on the Swiss Franc
    (C) Write puts on the Swiss Franc
    (D) Write calls on the Swiss Franc

28. Which one of the following is a correct statement regarding adjustment of an options contract for an odd stock split? The exercise price is:

    (A) decreased.
    (B) increased
    (C) unchanged
    (D) cancelled

29. An investor goes long 5 DEF June 25 calls at 3 and also goes long 5 DEF June 20 puts at 2. What is the investor's margin requirement?

    (A) $500
    (B) $2,500
    (C) $5,000
    (D) $1,250

30. Equity options have which of the following exercise styles?

    (A) European
    (B) American
    (C) Foreign
    (D) Australian

31. Which of the following is Not disclosed on a customer confirmation for an options transaction?

    (A) Premium
    (B) Contra broker
    (C) Number of contracts
    (D) Exercise price

32. Tyler buys 5 PQR Dec 45 puts at 3. What is Tyler's maximum potential gain?

    (A) $21,000
    (B) $22,500
    (C) Unlimited
    (D) $4,200

33. Which two of the following series would establish a vertical spread?

    I.   Long 1 MNO Nov 55 put
    II. Short 1 MNO Dec 60 call
    III. Long 1 MNO Oct 65 call
    IV. Short 1 MNO Nov 60 put

    (A) I and III
    (B) I and IV
    (C) II and III
    (D) II and IV

34. Narrow-based index options cease trading each day at:

    (A) 4:15pm eastern time
    (B) 11:59pm eastern time
    (C) 5:30pm eastern time
    (D) 4:00pm eastern time

35. Mr. Thomas buys 100 shares of IBM at $130 and also writes 1 IBM Aug 135 call at 4. Three weeks later, Mr. Thomas receives an assignment notice when IBM stock is trading at $142. What is the resulting profit?

    (A) $900
    (B) $500
    (C) $1,200
    (D) $1,600

36. Marc writes 1 GHI Sept 25 put at 3. What is Marc's maximum potential loss?

    (A) $300
    (B) $2,200
    (C) Unlimited
    (D) $2,500

37. A speculator initiates a position by buying 3 Mar 35 puts at 2. This is an example of:

    (A) an opening purchase.
    (B) an opening sale.
    (C) a closing purchase.
    (D) a closing sale.

38. A customer buys 1 HD June 35 call at 5 and also buys 1 HD June 30 put at 3. At what price does the underlying stock need to trade for the customer to earn a profit?

    (A) $26
    (B) $42.25
    (C) $40.50
    (D) $21.50

39. On July 10, 2010 the MSFT Dec 25 calls had a trading volume of 400 contracts. This is equivalent to how many shares of Microsoft common stock?

    (A) 400
    (B) 400,000
    (C) 80,000
    (D) 40,000

40. Which of the following is a Bear Spread?

    (A) Short a Sept 65 put and long a Sept 70 put
    (B) Long a Sept 65 put and Short a Sept 70 put
    (C) Short a Sept 65 put and long a Mar 60 put
    (D) Short a Sept 65 put and long a Mar 65 put

41. Which method does the OCC utilize in allocating an assignment notice to a broker-dealer?

    (A) Random Selection
    (B) Largest position
    (C) Smallest position
    (D) Oldest position

42. An investor buys 3 XL May 65 calls and simultaneously sells 3 XL May 70 calls. Which two of the following are correct?

    I.   Credit spread
    II. Debit spread
    III. He expects the spread to narrow
    IV. He expects the spread to widen

    (A) I and III
    (B) I and IV
    (C) II and III
    (D) II and IV

43. Which one of the following is a correct statement regarding adjustment of an options contract for a cash dividend? The number of shares per contract is:

    (A) increased
    (B) decreased.
    (C) cancelled
    (D) unchanged

44. In which of the following scenarios would a profit result for the writer of a put option?

    (A) The writer receives an assignment notice
    (B) The underlying stock declines in price below the strike of the option
    (C) The option expires worthless
    (D) The premium of the option increases

45. Tina purchased 500 shares of GHI Corp. at $50 and sold 5 GHI July 55 calls at 3. What is the name of this strategy?

    (A) Bearish call spread
    (B) Long strangle
    (C) Covered call writing
    (D) Bullish call spread

46. Paul shorts 100 shares of DDQ at $50 and sells 1 DDQ Oct 40 put at 2. Based on his positions, what are Paul's expectations of DDQ stock price during the life of the option? Paul is:

    (A) very bullish
    (B) moderately bullish
    (C) aggressively bearish
    (D) moderately bearish

47. Which of the following combined positions is bearish?

    (A) Short put + long call
    (B) Short put + short call
    (C) Long put + long call
    (D) Long put + short call

48. On January 2nd, Don purchases 1 GHI July 55 call and writes 1 GHI Sept 55 call. Which two of the following are correct?

    I.   Debit spread
    II. Credit spread
    III. Horizontal spread
    IV. Diagonal spread

    (A) I and III
    (B) I and IV
    (C) II and III
    (D) II and IV

49. An investor places a market order to buy a KO Oct 65 put which is trading at 3.25 - 3.55. Three days later he liquidates his position when the options are trading at: 3.15 - 3.30. What is the investor's resulting profit or loss?

    (A) $40 loss
    (B) $5 profit
    (C) $25 loss
    (D) $10 loss

50. Marty purchases 1,000 shares of XYZ at $50.75, and at the same time also purchases 10 XYZ Nov 50 puts at 3. In November the puts expire worthless and Marty sells all of his XYZ stock at $55. What is Marty's resulting profit or loss?

    (A) $5,000 profit
    (B) $4,250 profit
    (C) -$3,750 loss
    (D) $1,250 profit

OPTIONS EXPLANATIONS 10

1. **(A)**

This is an "Except" question. Meaning, three of the four choices are true statements. So, the correct answer is the statement which is incorrect. The straddle writer expects "neutrality" or "lack of volatility". Stated another way, straddle writers are neither bullish nor bearish, but expect the stock to stay in a narrow range. Straddle writers have two breakeven points which can be determined as follows:

Strike Price of Call Option	+ Total Premium	= Upside Breakeven Point
70	+ 6	= 76

Strike Price of Put Option	- Total Premium	= Downside Breakeven Point
70	-6	= 64

The Straddle Writer breaks even at $76/share and $64/share. He will profit if XYZ stock remains between $76 and $64. At $63/share, the investor will lose money since XYZ stock has declined below the downside breakeven point of $64/share.

2. **(A)**

A customer is required to pay for the purchase of an option within five business days following the trade date or T+5. It is important to note that the question reads: "According to Regulation T". It is the Federal Reserve Board through Regulation T that requires customer payment within five days from the trade date. T + 1 (Choice C) addresses settlement between the clearing firm and the Options Clearing Corporation ("OCC").

3. **(C)**

The premium paid for purchasing the call is added to the exercise price of the call as follows:

Strike Price (from exercise of call)	+ Premium	= cost basis
$2,500	+ $500	= $3,000

For tax purposes, the customer has a cost basis on HRB stock of $3,000. Note the customer has not realized a capital gain or loss since he did not sell the stock or option.

4. **(C)**

Sally has created a vertical spread or price spread, which consists of the purchase and sale of calls (or puts) on the same security, same expiration date, and different strike prices.

5. **(A)**

Broad-based Index Options trade each day until 4:15pm eastern time. S&P 500 Index Options are considered broad-based options because it is diversified across industry lines. On the other hand, narrow-based index options also trade each day until 4:00pm and are limited to one industry or sector of the market. Examples include, CBOE Gold Index Options and CBOE Internet Index Options.

6. **(A)**

Rick has created a Combination which consists of both purchases or sales of a call(s) and a put(s) on the same security with different expiration dates and/or strike prices. The Combination buyer (like a Straddle buyer) expects volatility in the underlying security.

7. **(D)**

The investor has sold naked call options. While the position has unlimited risk, the question instead asks about the position's maximum potential gain. The investor maximum gain is limited to the premium received which is calculated as follows:

Premium	X Contract Size	X Number of Contracts	= $Premium
2	X 100	X 2	= $400

8. **(C)**

In determining the premium of a yield-based option, it is calculated in the same manner as a price-based option as follows:

Premium	X Contract Size	X Number of Contracts	= $Premium
3.25	X 100	X 1	= $325

9. **(A)**

Burt has created a Short Combination which consists of writing or selling a call(s) and a put(s) on the same security, and different expiration dates and/or strikes prices. This is similar in concept to a short straddle in that the Combination Writer expects stability or neutrality. Stated another way, Combination writers are neither bullish nor bearish, but expect the underlying security to trade in a narrow range.

10. **(B)**

With the sale of 5 MSFT July 30 calls, Raj has created a Covered Call Writing Strategy. This is a moderately bullish strategy in that Raj's profit is limited to a rise in the stock up to $30/share (the price at which the stock could be called away) plus the premium received. Raj also has the goal of reducing risk as this is a conservative strategy. The maximum loss is limited to the amount paid for the stock minus the premium received for writing the options. This is also an income-generating strategy as the calls are written to generate income in additional to any dividend that may be received for holding MSFT stock.

11. **(B)**

Tara has realized an $800 capital loss in the year 2011. We will now summarize the tax issues as it relates to this question:

*   Options are capital assets that result in either capitals gains or losses
*   Standard or regular options result in short-term capital gains or losses because the maximum life of an option is nine-months
*   If an option expires, a taxable event is recognized in the year of expiration

12. **(B)**

The investor will create a wash sale by purchasing "substantially identical securities" within 30-days of the sale. In addition to purchasing YUM stock, the following would also meet the definition of "substantially identical securities" for purposes of the wash sale rule:

- YUM convertible preferred stock
- YUM convertible bonds
- YUM warrants
- YUM rights
- YUM call options (Choice B)

All of the above securities give the investor the ability to purchase YUM stock at a predetermined price.

13. **(B)**

The sale of a naked or uncovered put is the only one of the four strategies which has limited risk. The term naked or uncovered put means that the investor does not have cash equivalent to the aggregate strike price in his account. The sale of a naked put has limited risk which can be expressed as follows:

Aggregate Exercise Price	-	Premium	= $Maximum Loss

The investor may be obligated to purchase the stock at the strike price. If the stock declines to zero, the investor would lose the aggregate exercise price less the premium received. The three other strategies have unlimited risk for the following reasons:

- Sale of a straddle; embedded in the position is a naked call option, which has unlimited risk
- Short sale of stock; theoretically the stock could rise to infinity
- Sale of an uncovered or naked call option; theoretically the stock could rise to infinity

14. **(A)**

A long straddle has unlimited gain potential and consists of the purchase of a call and put on the same security, same expiration dates, and strike prices. A straddle buyer has unlimited gain potential because a long call option is embedded in his position. In other words, the call option gives Gary unlimited gain potential. While Gary can earn a profit from his put option, the potential gain on his put is limited since the stock can only decline to zero.

15. **(A)**

The purchase of narrow-based index put options would provide the greatest degree of protection for the energy fund. The portfolio manager would utilize the long puts as only an insurance policy to protect against a decline in his energy fund. Writing call options would only provide a slight cushion against a decline equal to the premium received. The purchase of narrow-based index put options are the more appropriate choice because the index is limited to one industry or sector of the market. CBOE Oil Index put options are an example of narrow-based index put options.

16. **(B)**

Greg's transactions result in a $1,000 loss which is calculated as follows:

Transaction	Debit or Credit
Bought 200 shares of ABC at $35	-$7,000 debit
Bought 2 ABC Feb 35 puts at 5	-$1,000 debit
Sold 200 ABC at $35 (Exercise of puts)	+$7,000 credit
-$1,000 loss	

17. **(B)**

Be aware that this is an Except question.

Long stock + short call should be identified as a covered call writing strategy which has both limited risk, and limited upside potential. A covered call writer will not benefit from a stock theoretically rising to infinity as the stock will be called away. In the event of a sharp rise in the stock, he will have the obligation to sell the stock at the strike price.

18. **(C)**

Time value can be expressed as follows:

Premium	- Intrinsic Value	= Time Value

So, given the premium of the option, we first need to determine if an option has any intrinsic value. The intrinsic value is subtracted from the premium; the remaining amount is the time value.

19. **(C)**

The position is a Protective Put Purchase, which consists of a long stock position and a long put.

Steve is using the long puts as an insurance policy to protect against a decline in his long stock position in RO. His maximum loss will be realized if RO stock remained at $45 or declined below $45. For example, if RO were to decline to zero, Steve could sell his 100 shares of RO stock at $45, Not selling RO stock at zero. This would be accomplished by exercising his RO put option and selling his 100 shares of RO stock at the strike price of $45. We can express the maximum loss of a Protective Put Purchase as follows:

Transaction	Debit or Credit
Bought 100 RO at $45	-$4,500
Bought 1 RO Dec 45 Put	-$300
Exercise of Put (sale of stock at $45)	+$4,500
-$300 loss	

20. **(A)**

A stock dividend is treated in the same manner as an odd stock split. That is, the exercise price decreases; and the number of shares per contract increase. Note the number of contracts remain unchanged for a stock dividend.

21. **(A)**

Index options settle on a cash basis. Since the customer is the seller, he is obligated to pay the buyer the intrinsic value (in-the-money amount) in cash. So, first we need to determine if the option has an intrinsic value. A put option has intrinsic value if the exercise price or strike price is above the market price of the underlying index. Since the put option has intrinsic value of 15 points, as the seller of the put, the customer is obligated to pay the buyer $1,500 which can be determined as follows:

Intrinsic Value	X number of contracts	X contract size	= $Intrinsic value
15	X 1	x 100	=$1,500

22. **(A)**

The broker-dealer notifies the Options Clearing Corporation ("OCC") that its customer would like to exercise his option. The OCC will use a random selection method to determine which broker-dealer will receive an assignment notice. The broker-dealer that receives an assignment notice will then assign its customer using a random method, first-in-first-out method, or any other method deemed fair and reasonable.

23. **(B)**

This is a bearish vertical call spread. The investor's maximum loss is the difference between the two strike prices
(-5 points) less the net credit of (+3 points). The maximum loss can be expressed as follows:

Transaction	Debit or Credit
Bought 5 XOM Apr 75 calls	-$2,000 debit
Sold 5 XOM Apr 70 calls	+$3,500 credit
Exercise of 75 calls	-$37,500 debit
Assignment of 70 calls	+$35,000 credit
Maximum Loss = -$1,000 (debit)	

24. **(D)**

Carol has created a Protective Call Purchase. This strategy is designed to protect her short stock position with the purchase of call options. Normally, we think of short stock ("selling short") as having unlimited risk. However, if ABC stock were to rise to infinity (theoretically), Carol would not have to go out to the open market and purchase the stock. She could exercise her ABC call option, purchasing the stock at the exercise price, and therefore covering her short stock position. As a result, Carol's loss of $8,000 is calculated as follows:

Transaction	Debit or Credit
Short sale of 1,000 ABC at $50/share	+$50,000 (credit)
Bought 10 ABC Dec 55 calls at 3	-$3,000 (debit)
Exercise of calls (bought 1,000 ABC at 55)	-$55,000 (debit)
-$8,000 loss	

25. **(A)**

This is an "Except" question. A short combination consists of a short call and short put on the same security with either different strike prices, expiration dates, or both. Embedded in a short combination is a naked call option which involves unlimited risk.

The purchase of a straddle has limited risk in that the maximum potential loss is the total premium paid for the call and put if both options expire worthless. Writing a covered call involves limited risk. If the covered call writer receives an assignment notice, he is obligated to sell the underlying security and the exercise price. Since he owns the underlying security, he does Not have to go to the market to make a purchase. The naked put writer realizes his maximum loss upon assignment and would be obligated to purchase the stock at the strike price. His maximum loss is the purchase price paid for the stock upon receiving an assignment notice less the premium received.

26. **(D)**

The Canadian importer will be making payment in U.S. dollars, which is not its preferred currency. The Canadian importer has a fear that the U.S. dollar will strengthen, or stated another way, the Canadian Dollar will weaken. As a result, the Canadian importer has assumed a bullish or long position in the Canadian Dollar. The best way to hedge this exposure is to assume bearish options on the Canadian Dollar. Bearish positions on the Canadian Dollar are the purchase of Canadian Dollar puts and the sale of Canadian Dollar calls.

27. **(B)**

Tag Heuer as a Swiss exporter will be receiving payment in U.S. dollars, which is not its preferred currency. The fear is that the U.S. dollar will weaken, or stated another way, the Swiss Franc will strengthen. Since Tag Heuer will assume a bullish position in the Swiss Franc, the best way to protect or hedge its position is to purchase calls on the Swiss Franc.

The purchase of calls on the Swiss Franc offers unlimited protection in the event of a sharp rise in the Swiss Franc. While writing puts on the Swiss Franc is also a bullish position, the protection offered is limited to the premium received.

28. **(A)**

An odd stock split is treated in the same manner as a stock dividend. That is, the exercise price decreases; and the number of shares per contract increase. Note the number of contracts remain unchanged for a stock dividend.

29. **(B)**

The investor has created a long combination which consists of a long call and a long put with either different expiration dates and/or strike prices. The Regulation T margin requirement is 100% of the premium of the calls and the puts which is calculated as follows:

Premium	X Contract Size	X Number of Contracts	= $ Premium
3	X 100	X 5	= $1,500
2	X 100	X 5	= $1,000
Total Premium = $2,500			

30. **(B)**

All equity options follow an American Style exercise. This means the holder of the option has the right to exercise the option on any day prior to expiration. This contrasts with a European Style exercise in which the holder may only exercise the option at one specific point in time, usually the day prior to expiration.

31. **(B)**

The contra broker to the transaction is not disclosed on a customer confirmation as it would not be relevant from the customer's prospective. However, the following information would be disclosed on a customer confirmation:

- Purchase or sale
- Series
    - underlying (security, currency, or index)
    - expiration date
    - strike price
    - call or put
- Premium

32. **(A)**

As the buyer of a put, Tyler's maximum potential gain would be realized if PQR declines to zero. If the market for PQR fell to zero, Tyler could buy the stock at $0/share, and exercise his put, putting or selling the stock at the strike price of $45/share. Tyler's profit would be 45 points less the 3-point premium paid for the puts or $1,500. To summarize, the maximum gain for the purchaser of a put can be determined as follows:

Aggregate Strike Price	- Premium	= Maximum Gain
$22,500	- $1,500	= $21,000

33. **(B)**

A vertical spread is established by the purchase (long) and sale (short) of either calls or puts on the same security, same expiration dates, but different strike prices. Choice B satisfies this criteria. Now let us go through a process of elimination to understand why the other choices do Not satisfy this criteria:

- Choice A – Involves two long positions, different expiration dates, and a put and a call
- Choice C – Involves different expiration dates
- Choice D – Involves two short positions, different expiration dates, and call and a put

34. **(D)**

Narrow-based index options are limited to one industry or sector of the market. Examples include, CBOE Gold Index Options and CBOE Internet Index Options. Narrow-based options trade each day until 4:00pm eastern time.

Broad-based index options, on the other hand, trade each day until 4:15pm eastern time. S&P 500 Index Options are considered broad-based options because it is diversified across industry lines.

35. (A)

Mr. Thomas earns a profit of $900 which can be determined as follows:

Transaction	Debit or Credit
Bought 100 IBM at $130/share	-$13,000 debit
Wrote 1 IBM Aug 135 call at 4	+$400 credit
Assignment of call – obligation to sell IBM at 135	+$13,500 credit
+$900 Profit	

36. (B)

As the writer of a put, Marc's maximum potential loss would be realized if GHI declines to zero. If the market for GHI declined to zero, Marc would be obligated to buy the stock at $25/share (assignment notice) when the stock is at $0/share worthless. Marc's loss would be 25 points less the 3-point premium received for writing the option. To summarize, the maximum loss for the writer of a put can be determined as follows:

Aggregate Assignment	- Premium	= Maximum Gain
$2,500	- $300	= $2,200

37. (A)

The speculator "initiates" a position with the purchase of puts. Initiating a position is synonymous with "opening" a position. Since he initiates a position with a buy or purchase, it is an "opening purchase". To liquidate his existing position, the speculator would need to engage in a closing transaction. Since he initially "bought" or a put, he would now need to sell a put option. This would require a 'closing sale". It is important to remember that liquidating is synonymous with closing. However, liquidating may require the sale or purchase. So, liquidating an existing position would be a 'closing sale" or a 'closing purchase".

38. (D)

You should be able to identify the position as a Long Combination. The combination buyer is long both a call and a put on the same security, same expiration dates, but different strike prices. The combination buyer, like the straddle buyer expects "volatility" in the underlying security. Stated another way, combination buyers are neither bullish nor bearish, but expect the stock to fluctuate in a wide range. Combination buyers have two breakeven points. While this question asks where the customer will earn a profit, we need to approach this question by determining the two breakeven points first. The breakeven points can be determined as follows:

Strike Price of Call Option	+ Total Debit	= Breakeven
35	+ 8	= 43

Strike Price of Put Option	- Total Debit	= Breakeven
30	+ 8	= 22

The customer will earn a profit if HD stock trades above $43/share (upside breakeven) or below $22/share. Since only choice D presents an answer that is outside of the breakeven points, $21.50/share would be profitable for the customer.

39. (D)

This is equivalent to 40,000 shares. Each option contract is based upon a contract size of 100 shares of common stock. Simply multiply the 400 contracts x 100 shares, which is equivalent to 40,000 shares.

40. **(A)**

A bear spread can be established with a short Sept 65 put (lower strike price) and a long a Sept 70 put (higher strike price).

Let us now take a closer look at the position:

Transactions
Short Sept 65 put
Long Sept 70 put *(dominant leg)*

Even though premiums are not given in the question, the put option with the higher strike would have a larger premium. We can now focus our attention on the put option with the higher premium or strike price. Since the investor has purchased a Sept 70 put (dominant leg), he is bearish.

41. **(A)**

The Options Clearing Corporation ("OCC") utilizes a Random Selection method when allocating an assignment notice to a broker-dealer. While a broker-dealer may utilize a Random Selection Method, a broker-dealer is also free to utilize a First-In-First-Out Method.

42. **(D)**

The investor has established a debit spread or net debit spread which can be determined as follows:

Transaction	Debit or Credit
Bought 3 XL May 65 calls (dominant leg)	**Debit (higher premium)**
Wrote 3 XL May 70 calls	Credit (lower premium)
Net Debit Spread	

Even though premiums are not given in the question, the call option with the lower strike price would have the higher premium or be the dominant leg of the spread. Focusing on the purchase of the May 65 calls (dominant leg), we are able to determine that the investor has established a net debit spread. An investor that establishes a net debit spread would like the spread to widen.

43. **(D)**

The number of shares per contract is not adjusted for cash dividends. It is important to note that adjustments to the strike price of an option contract are made for stock dividends, even stock splits, and odd stock splits, but not cash dividends.

44. **(C)**

Both put and call writers would like to receive the premium with hopes of the option expiring worthless. The maximum potential gain for both call and put writers is the premium received for the sale of the option.

45. **(C)**

Tina has created a Covered Call Writing strategy. The position consists of a long stock position and the sale of call options against the long position. Covered call writing is suitable for an investor with a conservative risk profile. This is also an income-generating strategy as the calls are written to generate income and is popular with dividend paying stocks. So, the investor receives dividend income from the underlying stock in addition to the premium income received for writing the options.

46. **(D)**

Paul has created a Covered Put Writing strategy which consists of short stock and the sale of a put. If Paul was aggressively bearish, he would only short sell DDQ stock. However, Paul decided to sell a put against DDQ stock which limits his maximum gain, as he will be obligated to purchase DDQ stock should it fall below 40 strike price of the put option, therefore covering the short stock position. As a result, Paul is moderately bearish.

47. **(D)**

Bearish positions consist of long puts and short calls. The holder of a put (long put) will profit from a decline in the stock, therefore being bearish. A call writer (short call) is also bearish as the writer of the call would like the stock to be at the strike price or lower at expiration, therefore benefiting from the option expiring. Examples of bullish positions include both long calls and short puts.

48. **(C)**

Don has created a Horizontal Credit Spread, which is created by the purchase and sale of either calls or puts on the same security, same strike prices, but different expiration dates.

Let us examine how we determined that this is a credit spread:

Transactions
Bought 1 GHI July 55 call
Sold 1 GHI Sept 55 call *(dominant leg)*

Even though premiums are not given in the question, the put option with the longer expiration date would have a higher premium. We can now focus our attention on the put option with the higher premium or longer expiration date. Since the investor has sold a GHI Sept 55 call (dominant leg), he has established a Net Credit Spread.

49. **(A)**

In the first scenario, the KO Oct 65 put is trading at: 3.15 – 3.30. The 3.15 refers to the bid, as this is the price at which the market maker is willing to buy the option. The 3.30 refers to the ask, as this is the price at which the market maker is willing to sell the option. Since the investor is not a market maker, he would purchase the option at the higher of the two prices (ask price), and sell the option at the lower the of the two prices (bid price).

Let us take a closer look at both scenarios:

Transaction	Trading	Price Bought or Sold	Debit or Credit
Bought 1 KO Oct 65 put	3.25 - 3.55	3.55	-$355 debit
Sold 1 KO Oct 65 put	3.15 - 3.30	3.15	+$315 credit
$40 loss			

50. **(D)**

Marty's transactions result in a profit of $1,250. Let us now see how we have made that determination:

Transaction	Debit or Credit
Bought 1,000 shares of XYZ at $50.75/share	-$50,750 debit
Bought 10 XYZ Nov 50 puts at 3	-$3,000 debit
Sold 1,000 XYZ at $55	+$55,000 credit
$1,250 profit	

21100283R00102

Made in the USA
Charleston, SC
06 August 2013